WHEN THE LEVEE BREAKs ≋

THE PATRONAGE CRISIS
AT THE PENNSYLVANIA TURNPIKE,
THE GENERAL ASSEMBLY &
THE STATE SUPREME COURT

William Keisling

YARDBIRD

ISBN 1-882611-00-4 Hardcover
ISBN 1-882611-01-2 Softcover

FIRST EDITION, Second Printing

This book has been printed on acid-free paper.

Copies of this book may be purchased for $11.95 for softcover, and
$18.95 for hardcover, plus 50 cents postage and handling from:

Yardbird Books
P.O. Box 5434
Harrisburg, PA 17110

Pennsylvania residents please add six percent sales tax.

E-mail communications and orders can be sent to:
CompuServe: 74720,3242   Internet: 74720.3242@compuserve.com

Library of Congress Cataloging-in-Publication Data

Keisling, William.
    When the levee breaks : the patronage crisis at the Pennsylvania
 Turnpike, the General Assembly & the State Supreme Court /
 William Keisling. -- 1st ed.
        p. cm.
    Includes bibliographical references.
    ISBN 1-882611-00-4 (HC : alk. paper)
    ISBN 1-882611-01-2 (pbk.: alk. paper)
        1. Political corruption--Pennsylvania. 2. Patronage, Political-
 -Pennsylvania. 3. Political corruption--United States.
    4. Patronage, Political--United States.   I. Title.
 JK3645.K38 1993
 320.9748--dc20
                                                    93-5117
                                                      CIP

Index

Dedicated to the memory of Thomas Jefferson

Part 1: ≈≈≈

Mokita on the Susquehanna

mokita — *New Guinean word for the truth everyone knows but no one speaks*

As I went walking that ribbon of highway
I saw above me the endless skyway
I saw below me the golden valley
This land was made for you and me.
　　　　— Woody Guthrie

Where goeth thou America in thy shiny car in the night?
　　　　— Jack Kerouac

1
Mail Call

It came in the mail without a return address. A plain brown envelope, my address typed on a white label. Only a hint of its origin — a postmark from Harrisburg, Pennsylvania. Inside, an anonymous letter, obviously written by a mid-level employee of the Pennsylvania Turnpike Commission. The missive somehow reminded me of a complaint letter you'd have found in a Soviet newspaper before the recent revolution.

The Pennsylvania Turnpike Commission, the anonymous writer explained, is a semi-independent commonwealth agency that administers the Pennsylvania turnpike. Five members govern the commission. The secretary of highways (the head of Pennsylvania's Department of Transportation, or PennDot) is the chairman. The governor of Pennsylvania appoints the other four commissioners — two from each party — to four-year terms. The state senate must approve these appointments.

The writer went on to complain of outright lawbreaking, waste, two-party privilege and politics at the turnpike. The complaints mostly involved that peculiar institution known as patronage. It seems that in June 1990 the United State Supreme Court ruled it was illegal for politicians and government administrators to hire cronies, friends or relatives. Yet the practice continued unabated at the turnpike, the writer complained. Girlfriends, brothers, husbands, sons-in-laws and other close relations and associates were still being hired left and right into well-paying turnpike jobs. Two patronage chiefs, one for each party, were still employed by the turnpike, the writer pointed out, though their roles now were illegal.

The letter went on to list other turnpike employees who the correspondent complained were lazy. Almost as if by afterthought, the writer alleged one employee was involved in a gambling ring. Some employees feared the turnpike had been infiltrated by organized crime, the writer related, and that "many... actually fear that the 'mafia' will rub out anyone who makes trouble."

2

Hallowed Ground to Dumping Ground

So someone at the turnpike had thrown a complaint letter out the window in the passing lane.

I'd never given much thought to the Pennsylvania turnpike. From time to time I'd drive on it, but not often, as I don't like to pay the toll. Back when I was a kid my grandparents used to take me for rides on the turnpike, marveling as they drove. This was back before I-81 opened, when they'd drive from their home in Scranton to Harrisburg on the turnpike's Northeast Extension. Before the extension opened it would take *forever* to drive to the capital city from Scranton. You'd take a twisty two-lane through the countryside (the scenery was great!) until you came to a little town, pass through traffic and red lights, before you were back on the two-lane. Along the way there were corny tourist traps and endless restaurants, hex signs and, as you neared coal country, fuming pink and gray mountains of stinking culm. Just as suddenly you might find yourself zooming through an iridescent stretch of cool road canopied by emerald trees. My grandfather used to talk about the speed of the turnpike, how it was now possible to drive from Scranton to Harrisburg *in less than three hours.* There was still a great romance about the turnpike when I was a boy. Today, on I-81, you can make the same trip in two hours or less. All the scenery looks the same and we don't think twice about how difficult the trip once was.

Today the romance has gone. A friend of mine who cleans up toxic waste told me the turnpike had a little-discussed environmental problem. Pollutants collect along the length of the Pennsylvania turnpike, from Ohio to New Jersey, he says. Unscrupulous truck drivers are suspected of cracking open the valves of their liquid waste trucks. They get on the turnpike, the whole while dripping toxic chemicals. By the time they hit Jersey and pay the toll their trucks are empty, the waste spat in a fine mist of toxic alphabet soup from Pittsburgh to Philadelphia. My friend said *he'd* never get out of his car and walk along the turnpike.

Over the years the turnpike became a figurative dumping ground of state patronage. Endless revenues from the tolls early on made it a cashbox for state politicians. Turnpike commissioners over time have had their share of scandal and prosecution. Pennsylvanians will tell you this isn't saying much, as every state agency seems to bubble scandal in bottomless reserve.

I became interested in the Pennsylvania turnpike's fall from grace. From hallowed ground to dumping ground makes an interesting cautionary tale. I'd come to see the story of the turnpike as emblematic of the state's rise and fall, and perhaps even America's. I'd come to see it as a story of a people who've lost touch with their roots, of unresponsible government out of control, of a road leading from a rich past to an uncertain future.

3
The People, Their Land, and Their Road

The story of the Pennsylvania turnpike runs through the heart of the story of Pennsylvania, much like the road slices through the heart of some of the richest land on earth. The people, their land, and their road share a common history. It is essentially a story of getting over a hill.

The Allegheny Mountains had always blocked westward movement. For a long time this barrier wasn't too restricting. Millions of acres of rich land east of the mountains kept pioneers happy for more than two hundred years. Still they kept coming, saying goodbye forever to loved ones, clearing the forests and breaking ground. Throughout the last half of the 1700s Pennsylvania's harbor city, Philadelphia, took them all in. In time Philadelphia grew to rival and then surpass Boston as the colonies' premier city.

Consider Philadelphia's ascendancy and you invariably find yourself considering the public-spiritedness of a single man, Benjamin Franklin. He founded the world's first subscription library. He helped the city create a hospital for the underprivileged. He helped establish the university. The fire company. The scientific society. He launched campaigns to clean and illuminate city streets. Franklin improved the postal service. (The British for many years ran a post office here, but it was too expensive, disliked as a tax, and there were privacy concerns, as the mail could be inspected for disloyal sentiments.)

Credit Franklin with increasing the post office's trustworthiness and efficiency. He shipped mail on the fastest ships available, hired more carriers and demanded they work nights. He was a businessman with a practical bent for making things work. Ever on the look-out for new ideas, he was a prolific inventor who never sought a patent for his discoveries, which included bifocals and the lightning rod. He preferred to take pleasure in seeing his inventions better his fellow citizens. This alone is inconceivable today, when the race for the patent is preached as being all important.

Franklin was a champion of thrift, hard work, and *human dignity.* His simple formula for success was to work a little harder than the competition. He was a world-renowned scientist who proved lightning was electricity. A successful writer and publisher. A skilled and popular diplomat. A septuagenarian revolutionary, fondly remembered for snoozing in the meetings of the American constitutional conventions. He counseled that if he and the others would put their shoulders to the big matters the little ones would take care of themselves. He persuaded the French king to aid America in the war with the British. He soon organized shipments of French matériel to the colonies, a service which historians say indispensably helped to win the War of Independence. The expense to Louis XVI ultimately contributed to the French Revolution. It's said that Benjamin Franklin of Philadelphia snatched lightning from God and scepters from kings.

By the end of Franklin's life Philadelphia had evolved from a dark, almost medieval town to the most advanced city in America. By 1800 Philadelphia was America's financial center and boasted the busiest port in the country. It would be easy enough to explain all this away by saying Franklin was a genius. For his ideas to take root they must certainly have fallen on fertile ground. The people must have wanted a better Pennsylvania.

The state, the country, the people all the while pushed west. By the early 1800s farmers had already cleared the rich lands around Lancaster and had settled well across the Susquehanna. Developing coal fields west of Philadelphia encouraged manufacturing. The commonwealth of Pennsylvania in 1794 opened a bumpy, log-covered turnpike that ran sixty-two miles from Philadelphia to Lancaster. (This road survives today as Route 30.) By 1803 this pike was extended to the Susquehanna River at Columbia. Still, there was very little travel beyond what was called The Barrier, or The Endless Mountains — The Appalachians. (President Thomas Jefferson wouldn't dispatch Lewis and Clark to explore The Wilderness until 1803. The same year Ohio became a state.)

In her 1950 book *The Story of the Pennsylvania Turnpike,* Penelope Redd Jones observes, "That the Appalachian Barrier, which can now be traversed over the Pennsylvania turnpike in less than four hours, was a barrier in fact as well as in name in the eyes of the colonists can be more readily appreciated when one realizes that from the time of the establishment of the British colony at Jamestown to the setting up of the first trading post on the other side of the Barrier 121 years had elapsed. That is how long it took the colonists to detour through 'The Endless Mountains.' In only half the time it took to colonize the Ohio Valley from the Coastal Plains, a distance of about three hundred miles, American pioneers had crossed the plains and the Rockies and were on the Pacific Coast."

It would be romantic to say that Pennsylvania at this time enjoyed a citizen legislature, with the public represented by farmers and workingmen. Already, in the late 1700s, Pennsylvania was perfecting a party patronage system. This was really the beginning of the age of professional politicians and American cronyism.

"Pennsylvania's reputation for political corruption is historic and enduring," writes state legislative historian Paul Beers in his book *Pennsylvania Politics Today and Yesterday.* "There never were any 'good old days.' Alexander Hamilton in 1794 during the Whiskey Rebellion dashed off a note: 'The political putrefaction of Pennsylvania is greater than I had any idea of.'"

Patronage in Pennsylvania was helped along by the budding federal government in the administrations of George Washington and John Adams. Tax collector and post offices, customs houses and other federal posts were filled almost exclusively by loyal Federalists, at first at the expense of Anti-federalists. Later, followers of Thomas Jefferson's Republican-Democrats also were excluded. In his book *The Federalists and the Origins of the U.S. Civil Service,* Carl E. Prince recounts the story of one Lord Butler, the postmaster of Wilkes-Barre. Butler "got in on the ground floor of emerging central and western Pennsylvania commerce in the 1780s acquiring goods imported into Philadelphia and selling them throughout the interior of the commonwealth," writes Prince. Using his growing wealth to buy into Federalist politics, Butler secured a seat in the state assembly and also became county sheriff. His counting house featured both the post office and the sheriff's office. Butler was "a zealous, almost fierce party man, 'decided in his political opinions and free in expressing them.'" When Jefferson became president his new postmaster general, Gideon Granger, targeted Butler for removal. "Butler informed the Republican postmaster general that he would neither relinquish his commission nor the office property in his possession, asserting that his removal was illegal," Prince recounts. Butler wrote the postmaster general that the real reason he wouldn't resign was that the job "encouraged my happiness whilst in no way affecting the happiness of any other being," and that this was "sufficient enough" reason to defy Granger. "Only the threat of federal prosecution brought the charade to an end," writes Prince, "and ended as well Butler's stormy tenure in federal office."

Pennsylvania seems doomed from this period on. Bad politics wasn't helped by the citizenry. The average Pennsylvanian — agrarian, self-reliant, complacent and endlessly practical — held on tight to a buck. "Pennsylvania-Dutch cheap," it's been called. Their representatives in the legislature kept in step with this frugality.

As early as 1760 calls arose for a Juniata/Allegheny rivers passage to western Pennsylvania. These calls fell on deaf and frugal ears. In the fall of 1790 one Daniel McClay laid out a canal route from the Stonycreek in Johnstown to the Poplar Run on the Frankstown branch of the Juniata. Enough popular support for McClay's idea surfaced that a legislative committee in 1791 recommended that the Juniata, Conemough and Kiskiminetas rivers be made navigable, with a portage laid over the Alleghenies. (See the 1992 National Park Service book *Pennsylvania Mainline Canal: Juniata and Western Divisions,* by David Fritz and A. Berle Clemensen. See also Julius Rubin's book, *Canal or Railroad?)* This far-sighted yet apparently expensive idea was not taken seriously by enough of the public, or the legislature. Had it been, Philadelphia today may have remained the premier American city, and Pennsylvania may still have been something.

This tendency to be penny wise and pound foolish set the stage for the singular event that cost Philadelphia and Pennsylvania their primacy. If the rise of the state can be tied to the career of one man, Franklin, so can its fall. The mayor of New York City, De Witt

"83"

Clinton, as early as 1809 began championing a century-old idea of joining the Great Lakes to the Atlantic. "Clinton's Ditch," as skeptics derided his plan, failed to win federal support. In 1815 Clinton spearheaded a petition drive to the New York legislature. This effort stirred up so much popular support that in 1816 a canal commission was formed with Clinton at its head. The next year, 1817, Clinton won the governorship of New York. In 1825 Clinton rode the first boat to traverse the Erie Canal. He celebrated the completion of the trip by pouring a small barrel of water from Lake Erie into the Hudson River.

He might as well have been pissing on Philadelphia. Within five years of the opening of Erie Canal, New York City had surpassed Philadelphia both as a port and as the nation's financial capital.

To the south, the Chesapeake & Ohio Canal threatened to send even more traffic through Baltimore. Seeing their prosperity slipping away, Pennsylvanians finally lunged into a do-or-die effort to throw flesh and cargo over the Alleghenies. Pennsylvania's state government in 1826 began construction of a rail and canal system known as the Main Line of Public Works. You'd catch a train in Philadelphia for the Susquehanna, ride a boat up the Juniata to Hollidaysburg, switch to a horse-drawn rail car over the Allegheny Portage Railroad to Johnstown, where you'd connect with a canal boat to Pittsburgh. All this took as much as four and half days, depending on whether horse or steam pulled your cars. Improvements later allowed you to remain in the same canal boat for the duration of the journey. Boats were hauled onto rail cars for the dry parts of the trip.

It was too little, too late. In 1839, seeing more and more commerce slipping away, Philadelphians persuaded the state legislature to finance a survey to find an all-rail route. One Col. Charles L. Schlatter surveyed three routes: a southern, a middle, and a northern. The middle route finally held the Pennsylvania Railroad. Such admired solutions as the Horseshoe Curve conquered The Barrier. In his book *Vanderbilt's Folly*, William H. Shank points out that "Unlike most of the other railroads of the 1840s, the Pennsylvania Railroad did not begin as a small, private enterprise, gradually growing to a position of strength after a period of hard struggle to survive. The Pennsylvania Railroad sprang into being suddenly, and with the moral and financial support of more than half the citizens of Pennsylvania. The PRR was the lusty child of a political battle which raged for four months in the state legislature at Harrisburg in 1846, concerning the future course to be pursued in Pennsylvania's east-west transportation planning."

Many western Pennsylvanians feverishly advocated tying Pittsburgh into the growing Baltimore B & O canal and rail system, on into Ohio, completely bypassing Philadelphia and the eastern part of the state. This scheme had the potential to tear the state in half and permanently damage state-wide development. The B & O plan almost won out. Shank's book recounts: "The B & O Bill was finally passed, but with a crippling amendment, which declared the whole act null and void if the Pennsylvania Railroad could raise three million dollars in stock subscriptions and actually contract for at least thirty miles of road (fifteen of them at the Pittsburgh end) before July 30, 1847." Perhaps sensing the B & O proposal could be the final blow, Philadelphians approved a plebiscite allowing their city to buy $2,500,000 worth of Pennsylvania Railroad stock. It turned out to be a popular stock offering, and the Pennsylvania Railroad was born.

The years leading up to and following the civil war brought tremendous growth to what was essentially Philadelphia's railroad. The PRR's rail tentacles soon stretched all the way to Chicago, to Washington DC, even to the hometowns of rival railroads, Baltimore and New York City. It became an era of cut-throat competition and speculation, when five rail lines ran to Chicago. At times you could ride all the way from New York to Chicago for a dollar. Speculators laid countless "nuisance lines" with the sole hope they'd be bought out by a big railroad.

This was the great birthing age of oil, coal, steal, steam and finance. Evolution begot the barons and the barons begot the trusts. Big-money largesse, legal and otherwise, flooded congress and state legislatures. In 1872 the Crédit Mobilier scandal rocked congress. Crédit Mobilier, a concern that oversaw construction of the Union Pacific Railroad, gained favorable terms for right-of-ways and land grants by offering half-priced company stock to prominent congressman. The paymaster of the scheme, Rep. Oakes Ames of Massachusetts, was a principal officer of Crédit Mobilier. Mark Twain, whose novel *The Gilded Age* gave the era its name, quipped, "I think I can say, and say with pride, that we have legislatures that bring higher prices than any in the world."

Newspaper cartoonists in this period characterized congress as controlled by fat trusts. Citizens' legislatures, if such animals ever existed, faded into idealized history as party bosses and wealthy interests explored new depths of corruption. There came a new era of graft and civic neglect. Philadelphia began to fill with slums. The area surrounding Independence Hall fell into seediness.

The thoughts of the barons and the bosses seldom turned to civic betterment. They acted for money, power, or out of pique, sometimes with unforeseen, far-flung results.

The story goes that William Vanderbilt, owner of the New York Central Railroad, offended George Pullman by refusing to install Pullman's patented beds in New York Central sleeping cars. Pullman and other similarly miffed industrialists backed a new railroad, the West Shore Road, to compete with Vanderbilt. In 1883 the new line began running up the west bank of the Hudson River, alongside Vanderbilt's New York Central, which ran on the east shore. There followed a year of cut-throat fare slashing, until the West Shore Road went bankrupt. Vanderbilt heard rumors that the Pennsylvania Rail Road was buying the bonds of the sinking West Shore Road. Foreclosure would bring the West Shore Road into the hands of the PRR, whose ever-expanding system would now include a spur up the Hudson, seriously rivaling Vanderbilt's line.

An angry drunkard might knock down a door. When scion William Vanderbilt of New York City got mad he knocked down the Appalachian Barrier. He proposed building The South Pennsylvania Railroad over what essentially was the southern route first surveyed by Col. Schlatter in 1839-41. Tunnels would give this route easy grades and short distances. The new track would run almost 10 percent shorter than the PRR's own cross-state routes.

Pittsburgh and Ohio industrialists formed a syndicate with Vanderbilt to build a fifteen million dollar railroad. These backers gambled on cheap fares from the South Pennsylvania and/or secret rebates from the PRR. Andrew Carnegie personally kicked in five million. Contracts were signed for nine tunnels and a bridge crossing the Susquehanna at Harrisburg.

Thousands of $1.25-a-day workers poured into the mountains to dig across the spine of the Appalachians. History tells us that the people are always eager to build, and almost always benefit. Poor leadership is often all that stands in their way.

Vanderbilt energetically pursued the project for two years, spending upwards of ten million dollars. Then rumors circulated that he wanted out, that perhaps he'd realized this new southern line might ultimately compete with his beloved New York Central.

Riding to his rescue came financier J.P. Morgan. Morgan had just toured Europe, where he'd found a total lack of confidence in American railroad stock. Morgan hoped to limit competition and so bring stability to the stocks. He planned a brokered peace between the feuding railroads, particularly the New York Central and the PRR. Pennsylvania Rail Road's president, George B. Roberts, at first wanted no part of a truce. He preferred to let Vanderbilt sway in the wind. Roberts boasted he'd "smash the South Penn like a bubble." In the end, on a hot July day in 1885, the belligerents met on a celebrated Hudson River boat trip aboard Morgan's yacht *Corsair*. A businessmen's truce ensued. The Pennsylvania Rail Road sold the West Shore line on the Hudson to Vanderbilt, while Vanderbilt abandoned his plans for the South Penn and dealt it to the PRR.

Notably absent from all these discussions were the public and government. This was the dinosaur age of free-roaming business tycoons, when *laissez-faire* government played little or no role in grand plans to build. The doomed South Penn Railroad, its tunnels and its gentle grades, lay abandoned for fifty years. The railroad to nowhere slept 60 percent complete. Only three miles of the total tunnel length had yet to be dug when Vanderbilt threw in the towel. Twenty-seven workers had died.

(Many of the same Pittsburgh investors of the South Penn, it's worth remembering, were members of a social club outside Johnstown, on the South Fork Reservoir. The socialites steadfastly refused to make repairs to the dam holding back their recreational lake. When the levee broke in 1889 a whole town was swept away, along with some 2,200 lives.)

Over the following four or five decades an occasional citizen would write to a newspaper or suggest to officials that some use be found for the nearly completed tunnels through the Alleghenies. A Somerset

County man successfully ran for the state legislature in 1908 with this campaign slogan: "Finish the South Penn Railroad and Give Hundreds of Thousands of Men Employment."

Over the decades the neglected tunnels filled with water. They remained an obscure, half-flooded curiosity from the past.

The total failure of businessmen, greed and financiers wouldn't come until the 1930's depression. Things were so bad that members of the State Planning Board in 1934 approached the Works Progress Administration, or WPA, with the idea of creating jobs by building a superhighway along the abandoned route of the South Penn Railroad. The Pennsylvania turnpike, we shouldn't forget, was created to make work.

Harry Hopkins of the WPA liked the idea so much that he sold it to president Franklin Roosevelt, former governor of New York. Two New Yorkers, then, Vanderbilt and, much later, Roosevelt, built the Pennsylvania turnpike. Pennsylvania no longer was the financial capital it was in the early 1800s, due in no small part to De Witt Clinton's Erie Canal. Pennsylvanians would subsequently spend a lot of time crawling to New Yorkers for money.

Financing the turnpike with private funds proved impossible. An initial $60 million bond issue was so poorly received that it had to be withdrawn. Penelope Redd Jones writes in her book, "The single New York investment firm to bid on the purchase of $60 million turnpike bonds discovered there was no market for the securities." Dan Cupper, in his 1990 book *The Pennsylvania Turnpike—A History*, relates, "The project's magnitude wasn't really the problem — the $35 million Golden Gate Bridge near San Francisco, a toll facility, was opened in May 1937. But, as one observer pointed out, bankers couldn't imagine a toll bridge 160 miles long. Nobody had ever built a toll highway of this length, cost and scale before, and it was not at all clear that it would or could pay for itself." Private investment firms didn't want to take a risk on the turnpike. Later, these timid spirits would benefit most handsomely from the toll road.

In the end, to make the project work, Roosevelt directed two New Deal agencies, the Reconstruction Finance Corporation, and the Public Works Administration, to respectively buy $35 million in turnpike bonds and issue $25 million in outright construction grants.

U.S. Interior Secretary Harold L. Ickes told the state turnpike chairman that Roosevelt's motivation wasn't merely jobs. Roosevelt saw war clouds. The American president thought a four-lane, limited-access superhighway over the Appalachian Barrier would greatly aid the flow of military supplies. By this time Adolf Hitler kept Germans hopping by constructing the autobahnen. To this day the degree of Hitler's influence on Pennsylvania's road system remains beyond the pale of polite conversation.

After almost a century and a half of public and private stumbling, high hopes to make jobs and dark fears to make war, Pennsylvanians finally got their road over the hill. Original turnpike projections promised to retire the road's debt in 1954. It was then to revert to the state highway system as a free road.

After all these years there remains the poetry of the Pennsylvania turnpike. The people loved their road, loved the idea of building it, of living near it.

To say the project was put on a fast track is an understatement. On October 10, 1938, the federal government gave final financial approval. The first contract was advertised four days later. Bids were received on October 26 and the contract was awarded the same day. Ground had to be broken the following day to comply with a the Public Works Administration deadline. God dwells in details: the turnpike commission didn't yet control an inch of right-of-way.

"We did not have a single acre of right-of-way at that hour," turnpike chairman Jones later recollected. "But through the efforts of the commission's general counsel, John D. Faller, the problem was solved. He rushed over into Cumberland County and related the story to the owner of a certain farm through which we had laid out the right-of-way and received permission to proceed.

"We drove out to this farm where 200 or 300 of the farmers and the neighboring people gathered on the spot where we turned the first shovel of earth. As we walked up the hill a lady came forward. Her name was Mrs. Eberly, the wife of the farmer on whose land we were starting. She had five children, ranging in age from two to ten years, clinging to her. She wanted the autograph of each member of the commission and of the PWA and RFC representatives.

"I said to her, 'Mrs. Eberly, why do you want these?' and her answer has been the inspiration from that day to this that has urged the commission on. She said, 'Mr. Jones, I want these autographs so that my children can say they saw history being made that day when the greatest highway, a new era of road building, was started.'"

We should keep in mind that Pennsylvania's politicians always considered patronage and jobs at the heart of the turnpike, even *before* its inception. "Because of the huge sums of money involved," writes Dan Cupper, "some back-alley battles broke out over how the project would be financed, and who would do the work." The WPA originally wanted to carry out the entire construction project, but the Pennsylvania highway contractors' group objected. The private contractors finally got the work. The awarding of jobs and the issue of who gets to award them are as much a part of the turnpike's heritage as the concrete that was poured.

Thousands of workers came into the mountains to work on the road. At least one of the men was documented to have worked on Vanderbilt's South Penn. So had one of the contractors — Mason & Hanger of New York City. Accommodations were in such short supply that some workers and their families lived in tents.

It turned out to be practical to use only six of the nine long-neglected and flooded tunnels. Crews instead dug one new tunnel and a record-breaking deep cutaway. Some close to the project later suggested that the mystique of using the abandoned tunnels had been more of a ploy to sell the project to the public than a necessity.

President Franklin Roosevelt may have had an appointment with destiny, but he didn't have an appointment to dedicate his child, the Pennsylvania turnpike. It was 1940, an election year. Roosevelt was campaigning for his controversial and unprecedented third term, and party rivalry kept him at bay. (When he'd attempted to pack the U.S. Supreme Court, opponents pointed out that Roosevelt sought more power than a good man should want, and more than a bad man should have.) The polio-crippled president ironically missed the one photo opportunity — cruising down the first modern super highway — that would have lent itself to his remaining in his car. "No dedication was in sight," writes Dan Cupper of the political delay, "and bondholders began to point out to the commission that every day the superhighway remained closed was another day without revenue to retire its debt." Cupper notes that commission chairman Walter Jones was forced to announce an opening date with "no ribbon cutting, no ceremony, no FDR." We shouldn't forget that the Pennsylvania turnpike, the blatant child of politics and patronage that it was, had no baptism. Roosevelt, the master politician of our century, chose to show political restraint, and demurred from attending.

In books and magazines we can still read about the poetry and romance of driving the Pennsylvania turnpike when it was new. Hundreds of motorists in cars and trucks queued up at the opening hour, midnight, October 1, 1940, to be among the first to drive, hitchhike and see the new road, to take their kids on it. Old fashioned bias-ply tires blew out, engines blew up, all unable to take the sustained high speeds of 75, 85, 95 mph and more. (There was no enforced speed limit.) A few motorists were so entranced they forgot to check the gas gauge and ran out of fuel. People were agog to see the future of highways. The smooth, four-lane divided roadway. The gentle grades and curves. The sweeping entrance and exit ramps. Then there were those futuristic, hexagonal toll booths. It all seemed like something out of the '39 World's Fair. Best of all, in the minds of some, were those stone service plazas encasing those sparkling Howard Johnson's. Could it get any better? (Howard Johnson's, by the way, subcontracted the right to operate its ten turnpike restaurants from the Standard Oil Company, which won the competitive bid for automotive and food services.)

People loved the road. An average of 6,000 vehicles rode the turnpike each of the first four days it was open. There were great traffic tie-ups around all entrances. The toll for the entire 160-mile route from Middlesex to Irwin was $1.50. The turnpike commission had expected only about 3,500 cars a day, while a more cautious U.S. Bureau of Public Roads guessed a mere 715 would pay the penny-a-mile toll.

Truckers loved the highway. It shaved as much as six hours, and

twenty gallons of fuel, from the old route. The turnpike proved endlessly easier and safer to negotiate over the mountains than the old ser-
pentine, two-lane, Rt. 30 Lincoln Highway.

All this seems like it happened not only in another time, but in
another world, peopled with friendlier beings than us. In late 1992, as
I visited libraries to read about the history of the turnpike, several
news stories concerning the road caught my attention. The magic
clearly was gone.

A national truckers' magazine, *Overdrive*, surveyed its 90,000 eigh-
teen-wheeled readers in 1992 and announced that the Pennsylvania
turnpike had been voted the second worst road in the nation. Only
New York City's Cross Bronx Highway was less liked by truckers. The
survey had asked the freight haulers to rank America's byways by
"road condition, congestion, etc."

This announcement seemed to rock the turnpike commission. A
damage-control news conference was convened. A turnpike
spokesman bristled that the simple explanation for the survey was that
the truckers didn't like to pay a fair toll. "It takes an unfair shot at the
commission and the state of Pennsylvania," Michael Kennedy, the
commission's deputy executive director for marketing, told reporters.
He complained that the magazine didn't put forth specific complaints.
"We don't do everything right, but if we don't know how to correct
(problems), it doesn't do us any good."

The intriguing question remained: why had so many professional
drivers given the turnpike a thumbs down? It was more than philosophical musing. Tolls in the 1990s earn the turnpike about $270
million a year, and even a 1 percent drop due to bad publicity could
prove disastrous, said turnpike executive director John Sokol. Several
expansion projects are underway, and there's more than a billion dollars in bond debt to be serviced.

No doubt part of the truckers' grudge is the toll. Since 1986 it's
increased 60 percent. It now costs your average five-axle, 31 to 40-ton
truck $79.95 to drive from Ohio to New Jersey, a far cry from the $3
to $10 truck toll for the 160 miles on the original road in 1940.

The commission fired back with conflicting poll results. A 1991
Pennsylvania State University poll of 829 people found 83.9 percent

of state citizens had a favorable opinion of the Pennsylvania turnpike.

My head swimming with poll numbers, I became as much of a numskull as these statistic slingers. I asked one friend why she thought it was so many truckers disliked the turnpike. She looked at me as though I'd become detached from reality.

"That's not hard," she said. "Why don't *you* like to drive on the turnpike?"

"I don't like to pay the toll," I answered honestly. "Not when I can take another road for free." I warmed to her question. "And the gas always seems much more expensive. And the fast food at the service plazas — Hardee's or Burger King or whatever they are these days — is always more expensive, and is always cold and terrible." Another friend volunteered that the road was lousy with cops.

Most of these complaints would be true of any limited-access toll road. Sensing some deeper problem, I began to notice popular dissatisfaction with America's first superhighway. People didn't seem to appreciate it anymore. They certainly didn't want to live near it. An article in the Philadelphia paper intoned there was such a weak market for real estate that properties near the turnpike and other major highways might not be good investments. Resale values along the turnpike might be down as much as 30 percent, the paper warned. Noise presumably was part of the problem. Tall concrete walls erected over the years to serve as noise barriers along stretches of the road don't help much, nor do they solve the marketability problem, readers were advised.

Not long afterward a Harrisburg television station aired an interview with a mid-state woman who was up in arms about a turnpike expansion project near her home. The road was already too busy, too noisy, and had taken too much land, she told TV land. What was the idea of expanding it more? The TV crew taped a shot of the road as seen from her house at night. A never-ending stampede of cars and trucks roared by. Where did they come from, where do they go?

I couldn't help thinking of the Eberlys, those starry-eyed farm souls who in 1938 had allowed the turnpike commissioners to celebrate groundbreaking on their land even though no legal right-of-way had yet been granted. Today those people would be locked up in the happy farm.

We are certainly a more jaded and jaundiced people than we were in those days. We are a lot harder to impress and wow.

The turnpike's deputy executive director for marketing says general griping isn't good enough, that the commission must have specific criticism to solve problems. Over the next several months I began listening to people who worked on, and drove, the turnpike. The portrait that began to emerge was of a turnpike commission that was politically out-of-control, oblivious even to U.S. Supreme Court rulings, living in a bureaucratic dream world, catering to the whims of greedy politicians and family factions, and desperately out of touch with the people it proposed to serve.

Those familiar with the Pennsylvania turnpike invariably complained to me about patronage. The irony wasn't lost on me. It was patronage, the awarding of jobs and contracts, that had built the turnpike. It was patronage, I began to see, that threatened to tear the turnpike apart. Patronage in the early days at the turnpike had been the building block. In the later days it has become its great stumbling block.

Over the ensuing months I spoke with many people familiar with the turnpike. Many worked on the road, or at the commission. Others had insights into its political or legislative history. Most presently worked for the turnpike while some had retired from it. Nearly everyone I interviewed drew a state paycheck. Some of those paychecks, I think it's pertinent to remark, were two or even three times the size of a paycheck drawn by an average Pennsylvanian.

Wanting people to speak freely, I paid surprise visits to their homes, in the evenings or on weekends. Many of those homes, I'll say in passing, were much more expensive than the homes of most of the Pennsylvanians for whom these state employees work.

One individual had a unique perspective of the turnpike and its relationship to the state legislature. He described the turnpike commission as presently enjoying a state of uneasy equilibrium. Its riches had been carved up and distributed among the state's various political groups. Between the Democrats and the Republicans, often referred to as the d's and the r's. "Thank God for the two parties," this man told me. He'd cite employees the r's wanted to fire, but whose jobs were protected by the d's. Factions in the state senate and the house had fingers in the turnpike. The governor's office even got a few people in, such as a bond counselor. Even so, I was told, other governors had been much more involved in the turnpike than had governor Robert Casey. Most agreed with me that Casey could be criticized for not putting enough of his own people in various agencies. Casey's predecessor, Richard Thornburgh, had made his presence much more felt at the turnpike. In some ways Thornburgh's presence was still felt. The former governor and U.S. attorney general still had friends in receipt of largesse, such as attorney Evans Rose, Thornburgh's former campaign finance chairman whose firm remained as a turnpike bond counselor.

I let slip to this insider that I was optimistic about the future of politics in Pennsylvania. A remarkable number of old-time state politicians were no longer with us. Most heartening of all, the public recently has shown a willingness to accept new faces. There was a clean slate, a chance for a fresh beginning. It seemed to me Pennsylvanians could be about to enjoy a long-overdue period of reform and change.

My conversant shook his head and said no, I was wrong. From his perspective, he said, state government was not going to reform and get better. It was getting worse, with no hope in sight.

We talked a little more small talk before my host asked the purpose of my visit. I explained that I had received an anonymous letter that purportedly contained information about the turnpike. He seemed unimpressed. He said from time to time a turnpike commissioner of one party might leak damaging information to certain newspaper reporters, thus "dropping a dime" on a commissioner of the other party. Some commissioner probably had dropped a dime my way, he suggested.

I said I didn't think that was the case. The letter in question contained damaging information on commissioners of both parties, I pointed out. It seemed to have originated from a mid-level turnpike employee who was fed up with the entire system.

I began to read from the letter, and my host grimaced. By the time I finished he'd confirmed most of it. This obviously hadn't come from a commissioner, he agreed. It had to have come from an employee, and it had the potential to cause the turnpike and the state legislature *lots* of trouble.

The most damaging aspect of the letter, I was told, had to do with the turnpike's hiring practices, which were blatantly and contemptuously in violation of the law. The United States Supreme Court in June 1990, had outlawed just about all political patronage hirings, I learned. The turnpike at first had tried to comply with the ruling, but the politicians in the state legislature had balked. The elimination of patronage was too much for the politicians to stomach. There was a bi-partisan revolt against the law of the land. The worst offenders, I'd be told again and again, were Republican state senator Robert Jubelirer (who at the time was president pro tempore of the state senate), and democratic state senator Vincent Fumo (who at the time was the ranking minority member of the state senate's appropriations committee). The turnpike commission was now deliberately and institutionally violating the law, I was told, and had set up an elaborate farce as a facade of compliance. So institutionalized was this lawbreaking and deception that most of the people I spoke with told me they'd be forced to deny everything if I called them at their offices and asked about it.

What was the name of the U.S. Supreme Court decision? I asked.

"Rutan v. *Republican Party of Illinois,"* I was told. It turned out that this court case had been filed against Republican governor Jim Thompson of Illinois by a state-employed rehabilitation counselor named Cynthia Rutan. Rutan for years had been denied a promotion because of her party affiliation. The supreme court, on a 5-to-4 decision handed down on June 21, 1990, ruled that not giving Rutan a job constituted a violation of her first amendment right of free speech.

I would come to learn that this ruling was despised and even laughed at by members of both political parties throughout the country, and particularly in Pennsylvania.

The ruling meant that nearly everyone hired or promoted at the turnpike after June 21, 1990, who was a political corny or a family member of a politician or a turnpike employee, was an illegal hire. There were *lots* of illegal hires, I came to learn. The ones named on the letter were just for starters.

The *Rutan* decision, I'd learn, had been meant as the last nail in the coffin of political patronage. Earlier supreme court decisions in 1976 and 1980 ended patronage firings.

Patronage hirings and firings, and the awarding of lucrative contracts, were historically what the Pennsylvania turnpike was all about.
A U.S. Supreme Court decision outlawing patronage on the
Pennsylvania turnpike turned out to be the bureaucratic equivalent of
the irresistible force meeting the immovable object. Old-timers were
betting on the immovable object.

The turnpike was a favorite of state politicians. The politicians
would see that contracts were awarded to friends. More often than not
the politicians would in turn receive political contributions from the
friendly contractors. Also at stake were thousands of turnpike jobs,
which the politicians for myriad reasons covetously fought to control
and dole out. Patronage hiring and firing was considered a time-honored tradition across state government, particularly at the turnpike.
Patronage was so institutionalized at the turnpike that, to this day, the
commission illegally employs two patronage chiefs, one Democrat and
the other Republican, who help to award party jobs, as alluded to in
the anonymous letter. Their official titles were the assistant executive
directors for the east (Democratic) and the west (Republican). Their
functions had been made illegal by the nation's highest court in 1990.
There they were, three years later, still helping to dole out party jobs.

This was not the first time the turnpike found itself at loggerheads
with the nation's high court. In the 1970s the U.S. Supreme Court
handed down its first decisions making patronage firings illegal, and
the turnpike patronage chiefs had balked. In the past, when one party
gained the upper hand over the other, the losing party's employees
were always purged. Tens of thousands of state workers used to be
thrown out. This *always* happened, as predictably as snow melts in
spring. The high court and unionization quickly changed the rules.
"What do you mean I can't fire those bastards!" the patronage chiefs
railed in the '70s. "Like hell!" They continued firing the bastards.

Lawsuits began flying. Those employees fired for political reasons,
in violation of supreme court rulings, had gone to court. They'd won,
and were reinstated with back pay. It proved expensive, publicly
embarrassing and ultimately futile to be taken to court for violating
the firing law. The patronage dons found themselves forced to comply. Court litigation successfully stopped patronage firings.

From 1990 to '92 the turnpike wasn't hauled into court over its

Rutan violations. This was at least partly because the new hiring and promotion restrictions as demanded by *Rutan* proved much harder to enforce. You have a good idea when you *lose* your job for political reasons. The opposing party comes in, you and lots of others get tossed. It's much harder to discern whether you've been victimized when *applying* for a job or promotion. An outsider who applies for a job has no way of knowing he's been passed over in favor of a less-qualified political insider. That's probably why there hadn't yet been any *Rutan*-based lawsuits filed against the turnpike, one administrator guessed, though he hinted that might soon change. Later I would hear a much more interesting explanation, having to do with the integrity of state courts.

Some of the public servants within the turnpike at first tried to uphold *Rutan,* I was told. These people soon were overwhelmed by the politicians of both parties and their operatives, who didn't want to lose control of political hiring.

The proof is in the payroll. The turnpike still employed the patronage chiefs, although their roles now were illegal. Samuel Carnabuci, the assistant executive director of the west, is the Republican patronage chief. Melvin Shelton, assistant executive director of the east, is the Democratic patronage boss. (Shelton is a crony of Democratic commissioner and Philadelphia party boss Robert "Bobby" Brady.) On May 29, 1992, Carnabuci and Shelton each received *identical* pay raises to $39.75 an hour, or more than $82,000 a year for both patronage bosses. (Both parties, we see, share and share alike.) Senator Jubelirer pushed his friend, Deborah Kovel, who was hired as assistant deputy executive director for fare collection. I heard continuous complaints that her previous experience had been to work in a diner. She was hired at a salary of $26.45 an hour, or about $55,000 a year. (Fare collection is an important patronage position because so many fare collectors are hired.) Executive director Sokol in January 1992 hired his brother, Thomas, as turnpike geologist at $21.63 an hour, or more than $44,000 annually. The turnpike never before had a full-time geologist. Also in January 1992, Republican commissioner Frank Ursomarso hired his brother-in-law, Walter Lawson, as director of purchasing at $30.29 an hour, or more than $63,000 a year. The brother-in-law had no experiencing in large-scale purchasing. Purchase orders started piling up. (I'd soon hear many tales of the infamous stacks of back-logged orders in the purchasing department.) Additional workers were moved into purchasing to help. There were many more, easily provable *Rutan* violations, I'd learn.

Not only were the politicians breaking the law, they'd constructed an elaborate farce to hide their law breaking. New hires were rubber stamped by a personnel committee, itself composed of representatives of the various political factions. The politicians had appointed friends and relatives to sit on a panel that approved hiring other friends and relatives. This procedure had been approved by a politically appointed lawyer, Peter Ennis. Ennis was given the job by Republican commissioner James Malone, turnpike employees say, as a favor to former state attorney general LeRoy Zimmerman. Zimmerman, upon leaving office, had himself been given a job in Ennis's law firm, Eckert, Seamans, Cherin & Mellott. Ennis's amazing role as consultant to the personnel committee, turnpike employees laughed, was to opine whether any politics were going on here.

The fascinating part of all this, I began to see, was the cooperation displayed by the two political parties when it comes to passing out the largesse. Schools might crumble, the swelling ranks of homeless might die of disease and starvation in the streets, banks might break — all while these windbags drag their feet in our legislature. The system never stops working and the good times never stop rolling for the inside political operatives.

The closer you examine the operations of today's government, the more the line between the two parties blurs, then disappears. Today's government, rather than belonging to us all, has de-evolved into a private fiefdom of the various clans in the governing class. They lobby, reward and regulate themselves. Nice work, if you can get it.

The bottom line, I came to learn, was that the turnpike hires some 120 employees a year, and awards hundreds of millions of dollars in contracts and bond obligations. The politicians weren't about to merrily give up any piece of this pie. The intensity of the bickering over the 120 awarded jobs can be understood by simple arithmetic. There are 203 members of the state house, and fifty state senators. Two hundred and fifty some chiefs can annually hire only 120 Indians. In this formula lots of mohicans are left out in the cold. The list of those excluded has swelled to include the U.S. Supreme Court, and the public.

At the happy hunting ground that is the Pennsylvania turnpike, patronage hiring and its resulting monetary rewards to the politicians is dime store stuff. The real wampum flows back to the pols from the countless contracts awarded by government — from supplies all the way up to extremely lucrative legal and bond work. The system — legal and otherwise — has evolved into an intricately inbred old-boy network that serves to keep insiders in, and outsiders out. It's called pinstripe patronage.

Things have gotten so bad that it's becoming hard to tell a deserving state contractor from someone's bumbling nephew.

A case in point, I learned, was what various employees described as the unfair representation of Syntonic Technology, Inc., in the anonymous letter I'd received. The letter stated, correctly, that Syntonic maintains much of the commission's electronic equipment. Its chief executive officer is Russell "Rusty" Lewis, who happens to be the son of nationally prominent Republican and former gubernatorial candidate Drew Lewis. The company previously had been owned by Control Data, and for many years was the only concern that performed maintenance on the turnpike's complicated and specialized electronic toll machinery. Lewis bought the company in 1985, state records indicate, while it was the only game in town. Now owned by a Republican family, Syntonic displayed political sophistication by sometimes employing former Democratic lieutenant governor Ernest Kline as its lobbyist. And so political lines are further blurred.

Over the years Syntonic was given turnpike work out of what seems like force of habit. I spoke with one turnpike employee who remembers sitting in on meetings when maintenance was discussed. "We'll give the work to Syntonic," a commissioner or director would say with almost a shrug. Then they'd agree to award Syntonic so many hours for the job.

Trouble is, this doesn't *look good.* It finally blew up on the turnpike and Syntonic. Someone "dropped a dime" and one of the Pittsburgh newspapers spilled ink on what superficially looks like a cozy relationship.

Embarrassed, the turnpike commissioners suddenly felt obligated to bid out the next maintenance job. One worker related to me with a snicker that only two bids came in — one from Syntonic and another from TRW. Syntonic's bid was the lowest. It won the contract.

Sometime later, Rusty Lewis of Syntonic sanguinely told me that he bears no grudge against the newspapers for occasional scrutiny. "The bottom line is that the press is doing its job and I understand that. We try to keep our head low, do a good job, and let the chips fall where they may." Syntonic, he said, "has been on the turnpike since 1938. There's nothing there and if there was it would have been ferreted out."

Syntonic charges a reasonable fee? I asked one turnpike employee.

"They're not cheap, but not abusive," was the answer. "They know enough not to kill the goose that lays the golden egg."

All this inbreeding of insiders, I noticed with some amusement, sometimes led to awkward semantics when discussing Syntonic (and others). How did Syntonic know what to charge? I asked.

"They have inside knowledge of—," this individual suddenly stopped himself. "Well not *inside knowledge.*" Inside knowledge has come to mean information provided by an insider, an illegal practice in government bids, stock transactions and the like. He explained he meant to say that Syntonic had been around so long they have an insider's knowledge of their industry. The work that's involved, the profit margins, that sort of thing. Their competitors were upstarts, outsiders, and so didn't know as well how to estimate a job. This kind of "inside" knowledge of one's industry, of course, is perfectly legal.

I bring up the point because I began to see there was a fine line everyone was dancing. That line was getting finer, to the point that you had to practically be a legal scholar to see it. The average person on the street might not see it at all.

One turnpike official allowed that the politicians and the commission certainly were consciously acting illegally where the *Rutan* decision was concerned. The real problem at the turnpike, he suggested, and throughout today's government, involved contractors. In a nutshell, the politicians had legalized bribery. Everybody knew what was going on, but nobody wanted to say it. Much as the Catholic Church used to sell indulgences before Martin Luther nailed his protest to the door, the politicians are giving no-bid state contracts to their friends and cronies, and receiving perfectly legal campaign contributions in return. Kickbacks.

It's worse than that. Many of these contracts are so lucrative that the contractors often obligingly give to every politician in sight, regardless of party. No one objects, because everyone gets a piece. Everybody's kept happy, the party keeps rolling, and nobody gets hurt, so the argument goes. Nobody's hurting but the public, which has no access to the party.

Politicians perpetuate the lie that "contributions" to them are voluntary. Even so the contractors, and even state employees, continue to believe, and more importantly to act, as though political "contributions" are absolutely necessary. The trick of the game has become to know which hat is important when it comes around.

Major contractors, for example, always seem to end up with invitations to political fundraisers. At the turnpike various employees, sometimes quite high ranking, curry favor with their political patrons by passing out the tickets. (The practice of government employees involved in political fundraising is supposedly illegal, but I came to understand it happens all the time.) For a well-placed politician, such as the president pro tempore of the senate, or chairman of the appropriations committee, these fundraising tickets are as good as money in the bank. For many contractors these "invitations to contribute" prove impossible to resist.

Ranking the "importance" of each invitation has become crucial. The ranking of fundraising appeals illuminates the all-but-unspoken nature of the dirty business. Contractors will often call around to trusted insiders trying to weigh whether such-and-such a solicitation from such-an-such a politician is "important." Several employees told the humorous story involving Democratic commissioner James Dodaro, who mysteriously involved himself in an obscure, local political race in western Pennsylvania. A prothonotary's race or something like that. No one understood why Dodaro wasted his time on it. It made the commissioner look silly, and those around him wondered about his political savvy and, it follows, his political future. Contractors soon received invitations from the commissioner to contribute to the obscure race. Mystified contractors telephoned around. "Is this fundraiser *important?*" one contractor asked a turnpike official I spoke with. No, he was told with a chuckle, it wasn't important.

It's important, of course, if your contract depends on it. You're paying the politician for business reasons, hoping you don't lose money. You're bribing the guy, whether anyone admits it or not. So long as the politicians declare the "contributions," and so long as they fall within the generous limits the politicians themselves have set, it's all perfectly legal.

This essentially dishonest and selfish attitude toward government has created a culture of greed and an ethical swamp. At the turnpike, and throughout much of government, I'd come to see that virtually no ethical standards exist. I'd find the entire system rotten with outrageous conflict of interest and petty nepotism. Just about everybody seems to have their own little hustle. People seem unwilling or unable to protest the excesses for fear they'll lose their own place on the food chain.

This bubbling stew of greed, kickbacks, conflicts of interest, nepotism, privilege and callus disregard for the law boils in a dangerous cauldron. In earlier years the turnpike had its share of criminal prosecutions. The supposed graft prosecutions of past Democratic commissioners Egidio Cerilli and Peter Camiel come easiest to mind. Both prosecutions involved aspects of patronage. Centuries-old patronage practices on which these men had built their careers came back to haunt and, ultimately, to destroy them. Both men died in 1991, Cerilli at age 66, and Camiel, at 81. Their passing marked the passing of an era. Their stories illuminate a patronage system in flux, and in crisis.

Egidio "Gene" Cerilli of Westmoreland County was either loved or hated, it seems. Many Democrats idolized him as a politician's politician. His fall began while he was working as a PennDot supervisor in Westmoreland County. Highway equipment contractors testified before a 1973 legislative committee that Cerilli and two of his lieutenants demanded kickbacks in return for state contracts. Testimony revealed that Cerilli and his men routinely and at various times picked up between $75 and $3,000 from the contractors. In all he was accused of collecting $8,300 from thirteen contractors from 1971 to '72. At the hearings Cerilli denied allegations of wrongdoing, while his two assistants remained quiet. The men were indicted, but the government indictment never mentioned where the kickbacks had gone.

The money went to the Democratic party. To the end, Cerilli would insist that the money represented voluntary contributions to Democratic campaigns. The time-honored system of collecting kickbacks from contractors had been operating so long that he perhaps thought it was voluntary. Both parties in those days routinely employed collectors to round up "contributions" from contractors. The unspoken irony behind Cerilli's prosecution was that the legislative committee which heard the evidence against him had been convened by ambitious and partisan Republican Cambria County state representative Patrick Gleason. Gleason's Republican family has controlled Cambria County politics since the 1920s. In the late 1940s they lost control of the county courthouse to the Democrats, led by boss John Torquato, Sr. Chairman Torquato would himself in the 1970s be prosecuted for demanding contributions from contractors and other public employees. It came out in Torquato's trial that the county Democrats' two collectors, Johnny George and Joseph Piurkowsky, used to work for the Republican Gleasons as collectors. When the Democrats won the courthouse in '47 the two collectors merely switched parties. Torquato was prosecuted by ambitious and partisan Republican U.S. attorney Dick Thornburgh, who let the statute of limitations expire against the Republican Gleasons before proceeding against Democrat Torquato. (Joseph O'Kicki, the former president judge of Cambria County, told me in an interview for my book *Maybe Four Steps* that he once ran a bag of cash, maced from public employees, across Johnstown for the Gleasons.) Cerilli's prosecution for old-fashioned collecting came about ten-years before governor Thornburgh would perfect the no-bid awarding of sweetheart contracts and the reciprocal, legalized receipt of political contributions. These days it's not collected, it's expected.

Many Democrats to this day consider Cerilli as having been selectively prosecuted. "He was doing what ten thousand other guys were doing," is how one old-timer phrased it. Another Democrat explained that Cerilli was good at bringing campaign money into the party, which was why the Republicans went after him. Strictly partisan, many say. That's not completely true. Several months after charges against Cerilli were aired in the legislative committee, governor Milton Shapp nominated him for a chair on the turnpike commission. Shapp said the turnpike needed Cerilli for his "expertise in labor-management relations." One of the first to publicly object to the appointment was none other than Democratic auditor general Bob Casey, now governor. Newspaper records show that Casey, in December 1973, wrote Shapp to say that the kickback allegations were reason enough to keep Cerilli off the turnpike. A court battle ensued, delaying the appointment, but Cerilli finally joined the commission in December 1974. He went on to become chairman, from which position in 1978 he was tried and convicted by a federal jury on the PennDot "extortion" charges. A convicted felon, he was forced to resign.

Cerilli remained a player in Democratic state politics through the next decade. He played a role in the state's biggest bribery scandal of the '80s. The son of fallen Cambria County Democratic boss Torquato was bribing everyone in sight to gain state contracts. Cerilli advised John Torquato, Jr., to "contribute" $100,000 to state auditor general Al Benedict and an unresolved amount to house majority leader James Manderino in return for a lucrative state social security recovery contract. Cerilli informed the young Torquato that he was the bagman for the prominent Democrats. The large contributions not forthcoming, auditor general Benedict soon reported Torquato to the FBI. That scandal ended when state treasurer Budd Dwyer, left holding the bag by these and other prominent officials, shot himself to death with a .357 magnum at a news conference.

These slights aside, Cerilli remained much beloved by Democrats at the turnpike. When Cerilli died in October 1991, a large mourning portrait of the convicted felon mysteriously appeared in the lobby of turnpike headquarters. More embarrassing, someone dispatched a state police honor guard from the turnpike's Troop T contingent to Cerilli's funeral. The presence of seven state troopers in honorary attire at the burial of a convicted felon created a stir. State police commissioner Glenn Walp ordered an investigation of the turnpike's

Troop T commander, captain Russell Clanagan, who'd sent the honor guard. A funeral detail required approval from Walp or his deputies, a state police spokesperson complained, but Walp was never asked. Troopers usually are assigned only to funerals of governors or other troopers, the state police spokesperson added. "No trooper should have been assigned to the funeral detail of Mr. Cerilli," the spokesperson warned. "Col. Walp is very serious about this."

The investigation of captain Clanagan was pushed under the carpet, one observer told me, when it was learned that Clanagan had been ordered to send the funeral honor guard by Democratic turnpike commissioner Dodaro.

Perhaps even more loved by state Democrats, and just as bedeviled by corruption charges involving old-time patronage practices, was turnpike commissioner Peter J. Camiel. Camiel was one of the more colorful characters in Pennsylvania politics. He certainly lived a life. In his youth he was a light-heavyweight prizefighter in Philadelphia. At nineteen he set out to see the country. He threshed Kansas wheat, poked Wyoming cows, worked as a longshoreman organizer and a theater stagehand in San Francisco. An expert crap shooter, one night, working as a stagehand, he won $3,600 from actor John Barrymore. Before long he drifted back to Philadelphia, where he was elected a Democratic ward leader. In 1952 he won a state senate seat in an upset victory, beating the brother of the Republican city boss. Time would make Camiel a millionaire wholesale beer distributor. He felt no compunction against using his public office to further his beer business. Once he fought a bill that sought to raise $37 million for Philadelphia schools when he learned the proposal levied a small tax on beer and liquor. In 1971 he won passage of a law allowing beer distributors a monopoly to import beer from out-of-state brewers.

Camiel became chairman of the Philadelphia Democratic committee in 1970. As Philadelphia boss he cut a deal with Pittsburgh Democrats in 1971 to nominate one of two open state supreme court seats. Democrats at each end of the state would select a candidate. Camiel picked Robert N.C. Nix, Jr., a black. Nix's father, Robert N.C. Nix, Sr., was the state's first black congressman, elected from Philadelphia in 1958. The Pittsburgh Democrats tried to balk at the prospect of running a black for supreme court, but Camiel held them to their agreement. Nix was elected and, by seniority, would become chief justice in 1984.

Chairman Camiel, meanwhile, deepened a feud with mayor Frank Rizzo. In 1973 he accused Rizzo of approaching him in the bathroom of the Bellevue Stratford Hotel and offering him control of the city's architectural contracts if Rizzo could select the next nominee for city district attorney. This episode tarnished Rizzo's Mr. Clean image, some say hurting his chances to become governor. Rizzo, in 1976, ousted Camiel as party chairman.

Hoping for a political comeback, Camiel won an appointment as turnpike commissioner. The comeback hit a snag with charges of corruption. On October 25, 1980, a federal jury convicted Camiel and two others on mail fraud charges. The feds accused them of placing thirty-six no-show "ghost" workers on the state senate payroll between 1974 and 1978. Convicted with Camiel were state senator Fumo, and senate majority leader Thomas Nolan. Fumo during some of the time in question had served as chairman Camiel's patronage chief, with the title executive assistant in charge of patronage. The three had written letters requesting jobs for the no-show workers, hence the mail fraud charges. Some of the ghosts ended up working at Democratic party headquarters while others didn't work at all.

Part of the trial centered on whether certain patronage practices may have still been legal at the time they were perpetrated. A city party official, referring to then-recent legislative patronage reforms, told reporters, "The case presented the thorny question of, 'When they did what they did, was it considered illegal at the time or merely unethical?'" It clearly was a case of old-time practices judged in the harsh light of a new day.

Camiel and Nolan took the jury's guilty verdict like rocks. Reports had Fumo, then thirty-seven years old, "visibly shaken" by the jury's decree. "I'm crushed," he told reporters as he left the courthouse. "I feel just utter despair." Even before the verdict Fumo was reported to be considering getting out of politics. Politics were getting too clean. Convicted on all fifteen charges brought against him, Fumo faced seventy-five years in the pen and a $15,000 fine. His electorate seemed to take it in stride. He was re-elected a few days later, but was not sworn in pending appeal. Governor Thornburgh had already suspended the indicted Camiel from the turnpike commission. The Philadelphia Inquirer, meanwhile, boasted about a series of articles it had published that it claimed was responsible for the guilty verdicts.

They appealed and, the next year, on August 4, 1981, federal judge Clifford Scott Green threw out the convictions. In response to pre-trial motions, Green acquitted the three of fraud charges, citing not so much a lack of evidence as conflicting evidence. Some of the conspirators and unindicted co-conspirators hated each other, Green ruled, so he found it hard to believe they'd cooperate in any scheme. (One or two of those involved had earlier deposed Camiel from the county chairmanship.) The prosecution had maintained there was one scheme, the defense said there was no scheme but if there was there were two unrelated schemes, while judge Green said evidence suggested there may have been as many as four separate schemes. Because the prosecution had developed evidence for one grand scam, the same evidence couldn't be applied to prove several scams, Green ruled, and dismissed charges. It wasn't exactly what you'd call a great moral victory.

The day after charges were dropped, the Inquirer, forgetting its earlier claim of proud responsibility for the convictions, ran a gushing puff-piece on Fumo. The paper described him glowingly as Philadelphia's wheeling and dealing "golden boy," who somehow now stood redeemed and venerated. When he heard the charges against him had been thrown out, "I let go a lot of emotion," Fumo told the Inquirer. "I cried for a while." Now a free man, Fumo brimmed with all the possibilities of a fresh start. He'd finally be sworn in for another term in the state senate. From here out he'd be a man of the people, a reformer, he promised. "There's a tax relief bill I want to get through," he bubbled. "Oh, there's just a lot of things, a long list." This wasn't Fumo's first brush with trouble. He'd resigned from his first stint in state government, as a commissioner in Milton Shapp's office of professional and occupational affairs in the 70s. He'd been accused of using that office to spy on Shapp's enemies. Even so, the Inquirer pointed out, no one ever alleged Fumo used his offices for "personal enrichment."

Things weren't so bright for Pete Camiel. Soon after the acquittal, turnpike chairman Jack Greenblat wrote governor Thornburgh to say Camiel would be reinstated as commissioner. Thornburgh objected, saying only he had the power to reinstate a commissioner. The governor said Camiel's acquittal, caused by a variance between the crimes charged and those proven by the evidence, "appeared to be based more on a legal technicality than a finding of innocence." Thornburgh cited a court ruling which, he said, empowered him to suspend anyone "for acts of misconduct that may fall short of an indictable offense."

Republican Thornburgh directed Republican attorney general LeRoy Zimmerman to seek an immediate court injunction to prevent Democrat party boss Camiel from being reinstated to the turnpike commission. There ensued a partisan battle in the state courts. Turnpike hands still talk about the partisan "battle of the house judges." Each party reached for its own house judge to overrule the other party's lower-court decision. (Republicans went to state supreme court justice William Hutchinson, while the Democrats used commonwealth court president judge James Crumlish.) Observers say this fight over Camiel was actually an attempt by Thornburgh to gain more control over the commission, particularly the awarding of bonds. While the court battle raged the commission lacked votes. Thornburgh deliberately worsened the situation by instructing his representative on the commission not to vote, creating a lack of quorum. Without a working panel of commissioners the turnpike was paralized. Day to day business like the processing of purchase orders and hirings ground to a halt. Fidelity Bank of Philadelphia, the turnpike's trustee, went to court to break the deadlock (some say Thornburgh encouraged the bank to sue). Thornburgh viewed the fight over Camiel as a bargaining chip to win more leverage (and largesse) in future turnpike battles.

This fight culminated with Camiel issuing vague instructions to a young turnpike lawyer to telephone state supreme court justice Nix after hours for an emergency order that would serve to retain Camiel as commissioner. Nix, nominated to the court by Camiel, was only too happy to help his patron. Justice Nix went so far as to suggest the type of order which the young, befuddled and shaken turnpike attorney would best request. (Not long afterward Camiel got his own lawyer; the joke at the turnpike is that chief justice Nix called Camiel to say the young turnpike lawyer didn't know what he was doing.) Camiel remained as commissioner. As we'll see, this use of "house judges" would set a bad and dangerous precedent.

Not illegal, but merely unethical, became the patronage battle cry at the turnpike for the next dozen years. There lately has been no successful prosecutions at the turnpike and, for that matter, throughout much of state government. This is not because those in government are getting more honest — by all accounts they're bravely crooked and getting braver. It's not only because our law enforcement community has been so poorly and politically administered for the last dozen or so years. It's mostly because we have created a political culture built on greed and selfishness. No one seems willing or able to draw the line between avarice and illegality. There are no standards by which to measure proper conduct.

When trying to make this point, many turnpike employees bring up the last attempted high-profile prosecution at the turnpike. Arthur Delinko was the turnpike's controller and chief financial officer, entrusted with handling the commission's investments. One day in 1985 a tip came in that Delinko was placing turnpike investments through a brokerage firm that employed his daughter. Several investigations ensued, and in late 1985 he was demoted to a consultant's position.

Prosecutors in the state attorney general's office came to allege that, between 1981 and 1983, Delinko had placed $1.3 billion in investments through three brokerage houses that had employed his daughter, Frances. The AG's office further alleged that his daughter and her partner, Alvin Dern, had split $738,000 in commissions from the investments. In July 1986, Arthur Delinko was indicted and charged with twenty-two counts of bribery and one count of racketeering. With the charges he was suspended without pay from the turnpike.

Trouble was, there was never any evidence developed that the daughter had returned profits to her father — which would have been illegal. There are certainly ethical questions about investing state money through one's daughter and making her a mint, but there are amazingly no laws on the books prohibiting it. (Delinko's daughter, interestingly, lost her job after this scandal came to light.)

Delinko told me the firms where his daughter worked may have received several hundred thousand dollars in commissions, but those commissions were split among large work groups. His daughter only earned, he estimated, perhaps no more than fifty thousand dollars from turnpike investments.

Anyone familiar with the nepotistic milieu at the turnpike might observe that Delinko was merely doing what everybody else was doing.

The trouble is, as I was saying, it looks bad. When the line gets so fine that only a legal scholar can find it, some legal scholar might try to find it. A politically motivated prosecutor — interested in going after individuals and not the entire corrupt system — might unfairly prosecute someone just because something looks bad. Often in Pennsylvania, in case after case, juries composed of twelve real-world people have thrown up their hands at the niceties and technicalities of the law and have convicted public officials simply when things look bad. Whenever a ruthless prosecutor can get a bad-looking case to court it often is trouble for the defendant.

Arthur Delinko's case never got to a jury. Dauphin County judge John Dowling threw out the case, but not before Delinko was run through the ringer a time or two. Dowling dismissed the case, he wrote in his opinion, because there was no evidence that Arthur Delinko had directly benefited from the investments.

"It must be emphasized that we are not dealing with the ethics of this situation," wrote Dowling, "nor whether it was fair or proper or judicious or even very smart for Arthur Delinko to do what he did.... We find the (state's bribery) act as interpreted to be unconstitutional and void on the grounds of vagueness."

Turnpike employees discussed Delinko's case with a tone of head-shaking incredulity. Various people, including Delinko, say they believe this prosecution resulted from a grudge harbored against Delinko by then-governor and future U.S. attorney general Thornburgh. One turnpike official described the turnpike under Thornburgh's tenure. One employee, he said, once found an illegal listening device. Many suspected that rogue law enforcement agents, wanting to kiss up to Dick, had planted illegal bugs to keep tabs on enemies. (Such paranoia isn't unusual in Pennsylvania state government. In late 1992 a squawk arose when Republicans in the state senate noticed what they considered to be an unusual wire snaking through one of their offices. They ordered the wire cut, fearing the Democrats had planted a bug. It turned out to be a computer line.) This suspicion that someone was planting bugs wasn't eased when Thornburgh planted his own law enforcement officer at the turnpike. Thornburgh's eyes and ears sat at a desk, day in and day out, intimidating everyone, not finding much. (Another turnpike employee countered that Thornburgh at least kept his eye on the turnpike and yelled loudly when he saw something he didn't like. This tended to keep people honest. No one is watching the turnpike these days, I was told, so there is misbehavior.)

Turnpike old-timers still recall the day the tip came in that Arthur Delinko was placing turnpike investments through his daughter. An internal investigation ensued. Thornburgh's pals in the prosecutor's office made up their mind to file charges. Turnpike investigators told the prosecutors it would be fruitless. Delinko's daughter was over twenty-one, and not living at home. It couldn't be proved that Arthur Delinko himself benefited from the transactions. There was no case and, I've been told, the prosecutors knew it from the start. Still they prosecuted, making some headlines before the case was dismissed. In 1992, as settlement for the ill-conceived prosecution, Arthur Delinko received $250,000 from the turnpike, and another $250,000 to cover his legal expenses. Delinko had broken no laws, so the turnpike had to pay for removing him from his job.

I asked Delinko about this settlement. He seemed to grow thoughtful. "I'd give it all back if they'd take it," he told me. "If I could take back all the pain suffered by my family."

This talk of possible illegalities led several turnpike employees and me to discuss the allegations of gambling found on the anonymous letter. One employee told me he knew of the individual mentioned on the disk but was unaware that he gambled. Another said there was simply a small football pool, "no big deal." One volunteered that this person did hang out with a second turnpike employee who was known throughout the department to have a gambling problem. Both were described as goofballs. One goofball, as luck would have it, has family ties to one of Pennsylvania's organized crime families.

Several employees advised me to go easy on these two. A gambling investigation, they said, was just the sort of easy, bullying case the state's prosecutors love. Great for publicity and headlines, yet offering little light on real problems.

One described the goofballs as easy marbles.

"Remember when you were a kid?" he asked. "When you played marbles you always picked up the easy ones first. They're two easy marbles. They'll get picked up first, and distract everybody from the harder marbles, the more important marbles."

He challenged me to go for the harder marbles. The harder marbles, he said, included several state senators, a few representatives, some bond counselors and bond underwriters. Maybe others. The real money at the turnpike was made by the people who put together the sale of the bonds. I would perform a public service, he suggested, to study the political contributions made by the bond people. That's the real big-money game that's being played at the Pennsylvania turnpike.

Was I aware, for example, that each bond issue unnecessarily requires at least two bond counselors, one from each political party? It was bad and getting worse. A recent bond issue had enjoyed *four* legal counsels, including Jim Flaherty, brother of former Democratic Pittsburgh mayor Pete Flaherty, and Evans Rose, the Thornburgh campaign finance chairman.

When one studies the game of marbles being played, one notices it's an insider's game. You could say it's a family affair. The turnpike's principal bond underwriter, described in all prospectuses as RRZ Public Markets, Inc. RRZ is short for Russell, Rea & Zappala. Charles Zappala of that firm is the brother of state supreme court justice Stephen Zappala. Justice Zappala was a former law partner and long-time friend with Democratic turnpike commissioner Dodaro. RRZ Public Markets, the bond underwriter, donates money to politicians through a private in-house political action committee called "The Committee for the Advancement of State and Local Government." Check out where the money goes, I was told.

Toward the end of our conversation one employee and I discussed how all these legal kickbacks serve to keep the recipients in office. We'd created a self-contained political class no longer in touch with the problems of average people. I expressed my support for term limitations, and suggested the salaries of our politicians should be limited to the take-home pay of the average Pennsylvanian. Let them figure out how to put more money in the pocket of the average person if they wanted a raise.

My conversant expressed opposition to term limitations. If you think things are screwed up now, the argument goes, wait till you put someone in there who doesn't care what happens five years from now, who only cares about what he can grab now. This seemed to me the situation we have at present.

This state employee became thoughtful and observed that politicians come and go, but the bureaucrats were here to stay. "They'll never get rid of us." I realized then the letter I'd received was sort of a stone thrown by the bureaucratic class at the politicians. Why don't you guys follow the law? the bureaucrats seemed to be taunting.

Patronage was on its way out and bureaucracy will reign supreme and everlasting, my conversant intimated. We spoke some about the pensions and the retirement accounts enjoyed by civil servants. Many politicians aren't around long enough to get a worthwhile pension. Did I realize that not even many newspaper reporters will get a decent pension? It was a big reason why many "seasoned" newspaper reporters go soft and kiss up to the politicians and the bureaucrats, he smiled. They want a state job before they got too old to collect a good pension. He laughed about a reporter working for the daily Harrisburg newspaper who he said was famous among bureaucrats for fawning for a job. "'Why doesn't someone just give that guy a pension?'" he said people would joke.

Then he became serious. He said the irony at the turnpike and throughout American government was that the *Rutan* violations, though against the law, were small potatoes in the big scheme of things. He said I should look instead at the lawyers. The bond underwriters. The special interests. The legal kickbacks. The politicians. The lax or non-existent ethical standards. Nobody seemed to be taking seriously this little-known ruling of the United States Supreme Court. He said he was sure, for example, that patronage hirings were as much a part of life as ever in the city of Philadelphia.

In fact, in early 1993 Philadelphia mayor Ed Rendell fired 123 workers from the city parking authority. Democratic turnpike commissioner *(and* Philadelphia Democratic chairman, *and* paid carpenters' union lobbyist) Bobby Brady said not to worry, he'd find them all jobs, as he controlled more jobs than anyone else in the state, he boasted. Brady's boasting was kicked around good-heartedly by the Philadelphia Inquirer, which never bothered to report to its readers that such patronage is now illegal. It's all just business as usual to Bobby Brady and the Inquirer.

"No one's hurt," my conversant said of the *Rutan* violations. He became suddenly thoughtful. Then he said, "I guess that's wrong. I guess the people who can't get those jobs are hurt."

5
Hell to Pay — Patronage in Crisis

Cynthia B. Rutan works for the state of Illinois as a rehabilitation counselor. She lives with her family in Springfield, the state capitol of Illinois, the hometown and final resting place of Lincoln.

She's had a state job since 1974. In 1983 Cynthia Rutan applied for a promotion. She was tested and interviewed, and was even chosen for the job by a supervisor. There was one last hurdle. Her application had to be sent to the governor's office for approval. She was denied the promotion.

This was happening to a lot of people she knew. The prevailing attitude, she says, was defeatist. What's the point of trying to fight the governor's office?

Rutan's problem was the result of an executive order issued by Republican governor James Thompson of Illinois on November 12, 1980. The order proclaimed a hiring freeze for every agency, bureau, board, or commission subject to his control. It prohibited state officials from hiring any employee, filling any vacancy, or creating any new position. Approximately 60,000 state jobs were affected, as well as more than 5,000 openings that became available each year due to resignations, retirements, deaths, expansion, or reorganization. Thompson's order stated that "no exceptions" were permitted without the governor's "express permission."

Requests for the governor's "express permission" became routine. Permission was granted or withheld through an agency created for this purpose, the Governor's Office of Personnel. Agencies screened applicants under Illinois' civil service system, made their personnel choices, then submitted them to the governor's office for approval or disapproval. Among the decisions requiring approval were new hires, promotions, transfers, and recalls after layoffs.

"By means of the freeze... the governor has been using (his) office to operate a political patronage system to limit state employment and beneficial employment-related decisions to those who are supported by the Republican Party," U.S. Supreme Court justice William Brennan would later note. "In reviewing an agency's request that a particular applicant be approved for a particular position, the governor's office looked at whether the applicant voted in Republican primaries in past elections years, whether the applicant has provided financial or other support to the Republican Party and its candidates, whether the applicant has promised to join and work for the Republican Party in the future, and whether the applicant has the support of the Republican Party officials at state or local levels."

In 1984 Cynthia Rutan applied for a second promotion. She was picked a second time, by a second supervisor. Again she was refused the job.

"It was getting to everybody," she told me. "These were jobs that were posted and advertised. But I kept seeing I was losing promotions to people who weren't even qualified." Her job, she says, is complicated — determining eligibility for Social Security — yet the state was hiring unqualified people who seemed to lack aptitude.

One day she decided to follow the procedure outlined by the governor for landing a job. She visited the appropriate party boss, and asked for a patronage application. She describes the application as ludicrous. How had she voted in the last fourteen primary elections? the form wanted to know. It asked kids how they'd voted. "It was ridiculous. For some of these summer jobs for kids — like a job at the state fair — most of the kids were fifteen or sixteen years old and couldn't vote. So they wanted to know how did your parents vote?"

Testing the waters, she asked the patronage boss if it would help if she gave money to the Republican Party. "Oh yes," he told her.

"How much should I give?"

"That's up to you."

Later she learned the going rate for the promotion she sought was $2,000 to $3,000. "I'd only get that much more if I got the promotion."

Cynthia Rutan had become a victim of patronage. She wasn't

alone. Americans have spent more than two hundred years wrestling with patronage. Patronage caused the assassination of one of our presidents. Patronage has been a snake in the garden since the earliest days of the republic. Its history is entangled in the roots of our two-party system. Patronage, and the debate over it, you begin to see, is at the very heart and soul of our country's history.

Patronage has been around forever, predating the Roman Empire. (Our word "patronage," of course, has its roots in the Latin *pater,* or father.) The Chinese are credited with having the first patronage and the first merit systems. Ancient Chinese bought and sold public offices as far back as 243 B.C. Mandarin status, the highest rank of Chinese civil service, required years of preparation and a tough examination.

Job selling rose to new heights in the Roman Empire when the Praetorian Guard began auctioning the office of emperor. The praetorians were higher paid than others, and even had their own set of legal privileges before the courts. They'd defend their privileged social order, and rid themselves of unprofitable emperors, with daggers and poison. They were finally abolished by the first Christian emperor, Constantine, in A.D. 312.

Patronage, oddly enough, was kept alive by the Roman Catholic church, apparently the first institution to sanction patronage by law. "References to it in canon law describe the practice as the benevolent exercise of privilege," write Martin and Susan Tolchin in their book *To the Victor....* "The term patronage was also used to describe the transfer of power by the Pope to his natural sons, euphemistically called nephews (hence, nepotism), and to his other relatives. 'Juspatronatus,' the sum of privileges according to canon law, was derived from the Roman system, which contained within itself an entire class of free men — not citizens — who attached themselves to patrons." A patron to the church was someone who financed the building of a parish, who in return was allowed to control the lives of some of those involved. "This included," the Tolchins note, "the occasional right to appoint lower clergy and, more often, to assign candidates who would take part in church ceremonies or enjoy certain of its privileges. After the Middle Ages, the ability of the Church to retain its patronage depended on its power vis-á-vis the monarchy. Thus early in its development, patronage became an index of the power of political institutions."

To make money, the bankrupt French and British crowns sold offices. An English Stuart might pay between 6,000 to 10,000 pounds to become secretary of state. Most offices were hereditary, though poor inheritors often sold their offices like stock on the open market. This undermined the loyalty of those holding the office. Those most able to pay weren't necessarily the ablest to govern. A bad administrator could sometimes spark a rebellion.

Upstart Americans quickly evolved their own methods of moving the levers of government. Parties and patronage weren't mentioned in the constitution, but the divisive debate over federalism laid the groundwork. By the time the constitution had been adopted, it simply seemed logical to put your guys in, and keep their guys out.

President George Washington at times pretended to disapprove of parties and patronage. His farewell address cautions against the formation of parties. In reality he deferred most matters of patronage and appointments to his secretary of the treasury, Alexander Hamilton, who nearly always appointed Federalists. Washington witnessed a growing rift between Hamilton and Thomas Jefferson. Jefferson's followers, the Republican-Democrats, soon were excluded.

The second president, John Adams, another Federalist, saw further factionalism in his own party eventually contribute to his electoral defeat to Thomas Jefferson. Adams made political appointments right up to his last day in office. One of his last acts was to appoint chief justice John Marshall to the supreme court. The Judiciary Act of 1801 allowed Adams to make last-minute appointments of more than 200 Federalist "midnight judges," who had no commission, duties or salary.

Jefferson disliked the idea of patronage, and preferred a merit system. By the time he was elected president, after twelve years of Washington and Adams, Federalists held all the offices. Jefferson observed that job vacancies "by death are few; by resignation none." Awash in Federalists, the pragmatist in him bailed the boat, tossing the opposition overboard. He systematically replaced them with his own partisans. His administration repealed the Judiciary Act of 1801, and informed the midnight judges to consider their appointments as never having been made.

William Marbury was one of forty-two justices of the peace appointed by Adams for the District of Columbia. He petitioned the U.S. Supreme Court to force secretary of state James Madison, by order of what was called "writ of mandamus," to deliver the commission. A section of the Judiciary Act of 1789 had empowered the supreme court to issue the mandamus writs. Mandamus, Latin for "we order," is a writ from a superior court ordering a public official, or a lower court, to perform a specified duty. This became the landmark 1803 case *Marbury* v. *Madison,* in which the supreme court under John Marshall struck down the part of the Judiciary Act of 1789 empowering the court to issue the writs of mandamus. The courts won that case: Marbury never got his job, and Jefferson was appalled that the court could overturn a law of congress. The Federalists still controlled the supreme court, and the Democratic-Republicans feared that the court's new-found power would be used to help the opposition. The Democratic-Republicans soon turned to the tactic of impeachment to check the courts.

The *Marbury* v. *Madison* decision set the precedent for judicial review of the constitutionality of laws. Today, when *Marbury* v. *Madison* is discussed it's usually from this perspective, and the decision's claim on implied powers. Often forgotten is that patronage was the cause of the decision. Our ongoing wrestling match with patronage is at the heart of not only our two-party system, but also the formation of judicial oversight and independence.

Jefferson, as said, opposed patronage, yet proceeded to use it. Thomas Jefferson was a walking contradiction. A landed aristocrat who fought for the rights of the common man, he often found himself derided as a traitor to his class. He wrote promissory words about self-evident truths of equality, and the endowment of certain unalienable rights, while he held slaves. He fretted over the tyranny of institutions, but created so many. He was an anti-federalist who used his executive power to double the nation's size with the Louisiana Purchase. Jefferson, the practical politician, proceeded to pack the government with members of his own party, so that by the end of his term most offices were filled by Democratic-Republicans. The strengthening of parties and their lifeblood, patronage, proved irresistible. Though all three wrote and spoke against the formation of parties, Jefferson,

Adams, and Washington can be credited with laying the groundwork for the spoils system to come.

It came full force in 1828 with president Andrew Jackson. "The people expect reform," Jackson told his political lieutenant, secretary of state and successor Martin Van Buren. "They shall not be disappointed." Hoping to shake things up by removing wealthy office holders, Jackson in time dismissed 2,000 of the federal government's 11,000 employees. Jackson's friend, New York senator William L. Marcy, immortalized the slogan, "To the victor belong the spoils of the enemy." Jackson insisted on personally overseeing all patronage appointments, a job he conducted from a pub called Gadsby's. One applicant requested a position paying $300 to $3,000 a year, anything but a clerkship since he couldn't write. By this time the spoils system was well established in states such as Pennsylvania and New York. The Jackson administration merely articulated, legitimized and introduced it unfettered to national government. (History also remembers Jackson as the only president to completely pay off the national debt.)

"Patronage, Jackson believed, could give the common man the opportunity to participate in government," write Martin and Susan Tolchin in their book *To the Victor....* "He was galled by the fact that one social class — the aristocracy — had monopolized public office for so long."

Patronage was so out of hand by 1841, with the inauguration of president William Henry Harrison, that upwards of 40,000 office seekers swarmed Washington in search of 23,700 jobs. Many office holders were incompetent, dishonest, or had no inclination for work.

Abraham Lincoln was one of the more adroit practitioners of patronage. Following his election in 1860 he kicked out 1,195 appointees to make room for Republicans, one of the more sweeping displays of patronage up to that time. In his day Lincoln was criticized for spending too much time doling out jobs, but historians consider its use vital in keeping the Union together, and a secret ingredient of his re-election. Most of the legions he put in office worked for him and the Union. Nevertheless he didn't enjoy fielding job requests. When he came down with a slight case of smallpox he told his secretary, "Tell all the office seekers to come at once, for now I have something I can give to all."

To become president would literally mean to become a moving target for office hopefuls. President James Garfield, having spent most of his time filling offices, complained in his diary, "Some civil service reform will come by necessity after the wearisome years of wasted Presidents have paved the way for it." By this time, in the early 1880s, the Republican party had split into two factions, the Stalwarts and the Half-Breeds. The factions wrangled mostly over patronage jobs and personalities, not politics. Garfield won office thanks to the support of the Half-Breeds. A Stalwart, Chester A. Arthur, won the vice presidency. Garfield repaid the Half-Breeds by appointing them to most of the jobs, passing over many Stalwarts. Awaiting a train to take him to a college reunion, Garfield was shot and mortally wounded by a disappointed job seeker. As Garfield lay bleeding on the platform the assassin yelled, "I am a Stalwart and Arthur is president now!" The aspiring job seeker won an appointment at the end of a rope.

This insanity finally shocked the public and congress into action. In 1883 congress passed the Pendleton Civil Service Act, which created a civil service commission to conduct examinations, and limited political interference. Cynical historians point out that by the 1880s kickbacks from office seekers no longer were as important to the two political parties, which now could rely on fat contributions from the trusts and smaller business interests.

The twentieth century was marked by various court and congressional efforts to keep politics out of the bureaucracy, and various efforts by politicians to ignore the same. The Hatch Act of 1939 (amended in 1940), limited the political involvement of government employees (in Pennsylvania this prohibition has often been ignored). Presidents trying to implement new policy meanwhile complained of an increasingly unresponsive bureaucracy. Issuing a directive, Harry Truman observed, was like "pushing on a string." Jimmy Carter tried to make the bureaucracy more efficient and responsive, in part by making it easier to fire civil servants.

Unionization and several U. S. Supreme Court rulings tore into state governments. In the 1976 case *Elrod* v. *Burns,* a newly elected Democratic sheriff was found to have unconstitutionally dismissed office workers and replaced them with supporters from his own party.

Justice Brennan wrote that the court in *Elrod* reasoned "conditioning employment on political activity pressures employees to pledge political allegiance to a party with which they prefer not to associate, to work for the election of political candidate they do not support, and to contribute money to be used to further policies with which they do not agree. The latter, the plurality noted, had been recognized by this court as 'tantamount to coerced belief.'"

In the *Elrod* decision the court cited among other precedents a 1972 case, *Perry* v. *Sindermann,* in which it held that a teacher was unconstitutionally refused a new contract by a school board "because he had been publicly critical of its policies."

Free speech and the First Amendment were increasingly viewed by the court as at odds with patronage. Coerced opinion, the court recognized, was unhealthy to a free society.

In a 1980 case, *Branti* v. *Finkel,* the court decided that the First Amendment prohibited a newly appointed Democratic public defender from discharging assistant public defenders who weren't Democrats. These two cases, *Elrod* and *Branti,* ruled out dismissing most employees for reasons of patronage, and set the stage for the next big hit at patronage, *Rutan* v. *the Republican Party of Illinois.*

One day while Cynthia Rutan was grousing about her inability to get a promotion a friend suggested she call Springfield attorney Mary Lee Leahy. As it turned out, several other state workers had recently contacted Leahy.

Rutan told me she was lucky to "find someone like Mary Lee Leahy who isn't interested in the buck but in doing the right thing." It turned out to be a long, bumpy road, taking eight years. They lost in court the first time out, then partly won an appeal. Word came that the United States Supreme Court agreed to hear the case.

Right up to the time when the supreme court verdict came in, Rutan says, she expected she'd lose. "I knew how deeply rooted patronage was in this country," she recalls, "so we knew we were taking on the big monster."

The big monster almost won. Rutan and four other state workers —a road equipment operator, a prison guard, a garage worker and a dietary manager — won the case, but only by a five-to-four margin. Justices Brennan, John P. Stevens, Byron White, Thurgood Marshall and Harry Blackmun sided with the workers; chief justice William Rehnquist, justices Antonin Scalia, Anthony Kennedy and Sandra O'Connor dissented.

"To the victor belong only those spoils that may be constitutionally obtained," Brennan pithily summarized in the majority opinion. "...The same First Amendment concerns that underlay our decisions in *Elrod,* and *Branti,* are implicated here. Employees who do not compromise their beliefs stand to lose the considerable increases in pay and job satisfaction attendant to promotions...and even their jobs if they are not rehired after a 'temporary' layoff. These are significant penalties and are imposed for the exercise of rights guaranteed by the First Amendment. Unless these patronage practices are narrowly tailored to further vital government interests, we must conclude that they impermissibly encroach on First Amendment freedoms."

A key argument in all this would center on whether the business of government would come to a grinding halt if the political parties lost control of the bureaucracy. The phrase "vital government interests" becomes a linchpin in these patronage decisions. It would be held that the government's "vital" policy interests could be met by firing incompetents, or appointing only a limited number of key, high-level political positions, such as a governor's immediate staff. "A government's interest in securing effective employees can be met by discharging, demoting or transferring staff members whose work is deficient," Brennan opined. "A government's interest in securing employees who will loyally implement its policies can be adequately served by choosing or dismissing certain high-level employees on the basis of their political views."

Will *Rutan* mean the end of the two-party system or democracy itself? Brennan, in his opinion, states that previous patronage restrictions haven't hurt the parties, or the republic. He recalls the *Elrod* decision: "The 'preservation of the democratic process' is no more furthered by the patronage promotions...than it is by patronage dismissals. ...Political parties have already survived the substantial decline in patronage employment practices in this century." Here Brennan cites the book *Goodbye to Good-time Charlie: The American*

Governorship Transformed by Larry Sabato: "'The number of patronage positions has significantly decreased in virtually every state.'" As well, *Congressional Quarterly's Guide to Current Issues and Activities:* "'Linkage(s) between political parties and government office holding... have died out under the pressures of varying forces (including) the declining influence of election workers when compared to media and money-intensive campaigning, such as distribution of form letters and advertising."

The really interesting arguments are found in justice Scalia's dissenting opinion, and particularly in an opinion concurring with the majority written by justice Stevens. The exchange between Stevens and Scalia ends up questioning whether the two parties may, in fact, be *bad* for the country. This debate seems like heresy when expressed in a lofty forum like the high court (it would be called fringe-thinking if expressed anywhere else). Their tiff over the propriety of the two-party system wasn't widely reported in the popular press. No use troubling the public with the thought that the two ruling parties might be complementary cups of poison.

Scalia begins his descent by complaining, "Today the court establishes the constitutional principle that party membership is not a permissible factor in the dispensation of government jobs, except those jobs for the performance of which party affiliation is an 'appropriate requirement.' It is hard to say precisely (or even generally) what that exception means, but if there is any category of jobs for whose performance party affiliation is not an appropriate requirement, it is the job of being a judge, where partisanship is not only unneeded but positively undesirable. It is, however, rare that a federal administration of one party will appoint a judge from another party. And it has always been rare. See *Marbury* v. *Madison.* Thus, the new principle that the court today announces will be enforced by a corps of judges (the members of this court included) who overwhelmingly owe their office to its violation."

Scalia seems to be questioning whether they are crippling the hand what feeds them. He launches into a defense of the two-party system, reciting a quotation from George Washington Plunkitt of New York's corrupt Tammany Hall political machine:

"I ain't up on sillygisms, but I can give you some arguments that nobody can answer.

"First, this great and glorious country was built up by political parties; second, parties can't hold together if their workers don't get offices when they win; third, if the parties go to pieces, the government they built up must go to pieces, too; fourth, then there'll be hell to pay."

This is a nicely colorful quote to find in a high court ruling. In many ways it sums up the strengths and weaknesses of Scalia's argument. Scalia is by far a better, more inviting writer than his fellow justices Brennan and Stevens, but his reasoning seems based on false assumptions and unthorough (and, one senses, even frightened) thinking. This country after all was built up thanks to its great natural resources, not the two political parties, both of which are arguably parasites at the fat picnic. To quote a member of Tammany Hall for his enlightened insights on the conduct of government is a little like asking Charles Manson to comment on the Scriptures.

"The whole point of my dissent," Scalia writes, "is that the desirability of patronage is a policy question to be decided by the people's representatives; I do not mean, therefore, to endorse that system...." He nonetheless proceeds to endorse the status quo for greedy professional political careerists. "A major study of the patronage system describes the reality as follows: 'Although men have many motives for entering political life...the vast underpinning of both major parties is made up of men who seek practical rewards. Tangible advantages constitute the unifying thread of most successful political practitioners.'"

Scalia cites the politics of self-interest and greed as something we'd be best learn to live with and accept. For the broad masses plagued by politicians and special-interest constituencies he says too bad, this is the world in which we find ourselves, and any antiquated notions of the common wealth be damned. Where politicians are concerned, he hypocritically waxes nostalgic for a better world. While lamenting that media and big money have high-jacked our political campaigns, he argues that patronage of yesteryear was a better system. "Increased reliance on money-intensive campaign techniques tends to entrench those in power much more effectively than patronage — but without the attendant benefit of strengthening the party system. A challenger can more easily obtain the support of party-workers (who can expect to be rewarded even if the candidate loses — if not this year, then the next) than the financial support of political action committees (which will generally support incumbents, who are likely to prevail)."

Scalia writes, "The patronage system does not, of course, merely foster political parties in general; it fosters the two-party system in particular." He seems, in a nutshell, protective of our two-party system, thankful for its fruits, and worried about tinkering with it.

The gloves come off and we get to the real mambo in justice Stevens' concurring opinion for upholding *Rutan*. He launches a frontal assault at Scalia's reasoning. Stevens seems to be tweaking the noses of the Reagan court appointees, of which Scalia is one, and their battle cry of a strict, "original intent" reading of the constitution. They say the constitution should be read literally and not reinterpreted by latter-day bench setters, yet patronage is never sanctioned by the document.

Scalia, Stevens writes, "makes the startling assertion that a long history of open and widespread use of patronage practices immunizes them from constitutional scrutiny.... Justice Scalia asserts that 'when a practice not expressly prohibited by the text of the Bill of Rights bears the endorsement of a long tradition of open, widespread, and unchallenged use that dates back to the beginning of the republic, we have no proper basis for striking it down.'.... The argument that traditional practices are immune from constitutional scrutiny is advanced in two plurality opinions that justice Scalia has authored, but not by any opinion joined by a majority of the members of this court."

Stevens cites a previous opinion in which he noted, "if the age of a pernicious practice were a sufficient reason for its continued acceptance, the constitutional attack on racial discrimination would, of course, have been doomed to failure."

Here, in a remarkable footnote, Stevens takes a direct swing (shudder the thought!) at the two-party system, and the hypocrisy of the Reagan appointed "strict constructionists" who support it. "Ironically," he writes, "at the time of the adoption of the Bill of

Rights, the party system itself was far from an 'accepted political nor(m).'" Stevens quotes a passage from Richard Hofstadter's book, *The Idea of a Party System.* "Our founders viewed it as a pathology: 'Political discussion of eighteenth-century England and America was pervaded by a kind of anti-party cant. Jonathan Swift, in his *Thoughts on Various Subjects,* had said that "Party is the madness of many, for the gain of the few." This maxim, which was repeated on this side of the Atlantic by men like John Adams and William Paterson, plainly struck a deep resonance in the American mind. Madison and Hamilton, when they discussed parties or factions, (for them the terms were usually interchangeable) in *The Federalist,* did so only to arraign their bad effects. In the great debate over the adoption of the Constitution both sides spoke ill of parties. The popular sage, Franklin (who was not always consistent on the subject), gave an eloquent warning against factions and "the infinite mutual abuse of parties, tearing to pieces the best of characters." George Washington devoted a large part of his political testament, the Farewell Address, to stern warnings against "the baneful effects of the Spirit of Party." His successor, John Adams, believed that "a division of the republic into two great parties... is to be dreaded as the greatest political evil under the Constitution." Similar admonitions can be found in the writings of the arch-Federalist Fisher Adams and the "philosopher of Jeffersonian democracy," John Taylor of Caroline. If there was one point of political philosophy upon which these men, who differed on so many things, agreed quite readily, it was their common conviction about the baneful effects of the spirit of party.'"

Stevens is saying that those who pretend to read the constitution literally have little understanding of the dynamic genesis of the document. Politics is a flowing river, not a stone tablet. Not to change simply because things have always been is to refuse a lifeboat because the Titanic has taken us this far.

The supreme court, in this discussion of the worthiness and appropriateness of our parties, proved to be well out in front of both politicians and the media. The national press generally greeted the *Rutan* decision with a smarmy tone, rounding up the usual suspects — politicians and "political scientists" — who for the most part issued bland reassurances that nothing much would change. A few good-government types were allowed to cackle that the decision marked a new day. A dejected governor Thompson of Illinois told the Chicago papers, "I think this will strike a severe blow at whatever is left of political parties in America." For the most part, to my ear, the press marked *Rutan* with yawning derision. Aside from Thompson's funereal lament, I could find no other hints that the parties of Jefferson and Lincoln might soon join the party of Lenin and Stalin on the trash heap of history. Just the opposite. We were reassured by the high priests to expect business as usual.

Former Illinois legislator James Nowlan wrote an article for the Chicago Tribune entitled, "Death knell for patronage? Hardly." "There will still be job patronage," he writes. "Bureaucrats and government union officials will continue to use their special knowledge of the personnel game to help their friends secure jobs and promotions." He cites what he calls the "new patronage." "...Since television has replaced precinct workers for the most part, money to buy TV spots has become the most important medium of the new patronage. Banks, law firms, investment houses, contractors and interest groups — those who do business in government and legislation — fuel campaigns with annual contributions of $10,000 to $100,000, often in the expectation of state business." (Thomas Nast and other cartoonists of the late nineteenth century, who regularly depicted the trusts as moneybags with overpowering, corrupting influence on politicians, would be amused by Nowlan's assertion that big money is a new patronage.)

In a New York Times article titled, "Why Patronage is Unlikely to Fade" (subtitled "An Ingrained American Tradition"), writer Martin Tolchin interviews several professors who snicker at *Rutan*. "The supreme court decision is going to be devilishly hard to enforce," one ivory-towered observer posits. Tolchin notes, "Elected officials can also place their supporters in jobs in private industry. The late mayor Richard J. Daley of Chicago was said to control 30,000 jobs in private industry — janitors, carpenters and electricians as well as corporate positions — nearly as many as his Democratic organization controlled in city and county government. Experts on Illinois patronage say the practice continues." (This trick also lives on in Pennsylvania, where turnpike employees complain that relatives of commissioners hold jobs with contractors.)

Taking the opposite view, the Washington Post quoted "political scientists" who said the decision is "likely to mark the end of the long-standing but waning American tradition of patronage." The Post noted that the decision came at a time when "many political scientists are arguing that expanding the patronage power of elected officials might make bureaucracies more accountable and strengthen belea-guered political parties." By coincidence, *Rutan* was handed down the same day the senate failed to overturn a patronage-related veto by president George Bush. Bush's veto prevented a weakening of the 1939 Hatch Act, which prohibits political involvement of government employees. They're still wrangling over patronage in congress. So it's too early to write patronage's obituary.

The Washington Post went so far as to dig up author Larry Sabato, political scientist at the University of Virginia. Sabato, it reported, "described himself as 'horrified and saddened' that his work had been cited by justice William J. Brennan Jr. in the majority opinion limit-ing patronage. Sabato argues that the elected officials need more, not less, political discretion." He tells the Post, "This is a very far-reaching decision. It's going to reach into the lowest and mid-levels of govern-ment."

Paul Tully, of the Democratic National Committee, was quoted by the Post as saying that "he thought the decision would affect political organizations in suburban areas such as Long Island, N.Y., and in some parts of the Deep South and some jobs 'tucked away' in some cities and state governments." The Pennsylvania turnpike would prove to be even more resistant to change, more "tucked away" than even the Deep South.

Another political scientist, Esther Fuch of Bernard College, was less convinced, telling the Post that local politicians were already "one step ahead of the supreme court. 'Many cities are hiring temporaries or provisionals when they want to circumvent civil service rules, so the decision may not have much of an impact,' she said. Referring to local politicians, she added: 'They're not dumb, these guys.'"

The Boston Globe ran a headline reading, "In Massachusetts, mixed reviews," beneath which Martin Linsky of the John F. Kennedy School of Government is quoted as scoffing, "It appears that it

(Rutan) means nothing. All it means: if you want to hire someone, you have to make a case for their competency."

All this mugwumpery is fine and entertaining, but, as I said, I was struck that I could find no mention in any newspaper of the court's debate over whether our two parties were unhealthy for the country. In this sense, the supreme court seemed to be one step ahead of the mugwumps and the wags, and in tune with the public.

Mary Lee Leahy, the attorney for Cynthia Rutan, told me all this grumbling about the enforceability of *Rutan* was just a lot of whistling past the graveyard. She said she was in the process of pursuing several punitive damage suits against *Rutan* violators. In Illinois the state doesn't reimburse those found guilty of employment violations. When individual supervisors feel the sting in the pocketbook, she said, illegal hiring should stop.

Might a hiring committee merely have to make a case for an employee's competency? I asked.

She laughed and said that was precisely the argument that had lost before the supreme court. "That's exactly the position the respondents took."

In certain states, she said, *Rutan* has meant a revolution in public employment. Following the decision, the Illinois state government examined 67,000 patronage jobs and ruled only 3,000 of them were exempt from *Rutan*. The remaining 64,000 would now be free of patronage. These jobs are now picked by aptitude or lottery, not political bosses.

"I think there are some people in Illinois who are genuinely trying to enforce *Rutan*," she said, "and others who are not."

As predicted by some, the latest trick of those trying to get around the law in Illinois is to hire workers on six-month, non-renewable retainers. The first time a worker came to Leahy complaining of this she said she thought it was a fluke. Soon she learned some 1,400 highway workers had been hired on six-month retainers. This not only violates the spirit of *Rutan*, she said, it subverts the personnel code. Six-month jobs have no benefits.

She plans more court action to fight infractions. Ignoring *Rutan* could prove politically embarrassing, she said. The governor and others have sworn to uphold the law.

Leahy expressed interest in the *Rutan* violations in Pennsylvania. She said her husband, when they were researching the case, had identified Pennsylvania as one of the states with a historically bad patronage problem. The other problem states, she found, were Massachusetts, West Virginia and Illinois. Many states west of the Mississippi, such as Wisconsin and Minnesota, were blessed with good-government crusades at the start of the century. Those states now find themselves remarkably free of patronage. One Californian told Leahy he was amazed at the extent of patronage in the East.

Why was patronage such a bad thing? I asked her. Patronage, she said, was bad for efficiency and kept the most competent from getting a job.

Cynthia Rutan and the four other plaintiffs in the case got their promotions. In a fairness hearing in April 1992, each also was awarded a $6,000 settlement from the state of Illinois.

I asked Rutan whether she was concerned about the impact the decision might have on the two-party system. "Everybody was so fed up we didn't care about the two-party system," she laughed. Let the best workers be hired, she said, and let the public vote for the best candidates, regardless of party.

When she spoke with me about the decision that came to bear her name, Rutan seemed to bubble. After the decision was handed down she'd experienced a few humorous incidents at work. In January 1991, while she was filling-in temporarily for a supervisor, she and others were called to a meeting where they received *"Rutan* training" from a higher-up. The supervisor began lecturing to Rutan on *Rutan.* The others turned in their seats to look at the woman who'd changed the law.

Rutan, like attorney Leahy, was interested in *Rutan* violations at the Pennsylvania turnpike. I listed some examples of husbands, girlfriends, relatives and cronies who'd been given jobs and promotions. Yes, Rutan laughed, they were all *Rutan* violations. She encouraged Pennsylvania public employees to come together and fight. "But if all you want to do is stand around the water cooler and whine then forget it."

Gather evidence, keep eyes and ears open, was her advice. The patronage form that the Illinois Republican Party had asked her to fill out ended up as an exhibit before the U. S. Supreme Court.

"One thing I've learned from all this is that there isn't one thing that isn't important. Write down everything you hear."

She said one of her co-workers overheard a party operative demanding $50 from a doctor, threatening not to renew the doctor's state contract if he didn't "contribute." A local newspaper got ahold of that story and created bad publicity for the state.

"There's strength in numbers," she says. "Band together. They can't find excuses to fire four or five of you, like they can fire a single worker. It really does intimidate them."

She said supervisors who violate *Rutan* are liable to have their personal assets attached by the courts.

"They cut me a wide path at work, now."

6
Keeping Patronage Alive

The Pennsylvania turnpike was proposed in the 1930s to create jobs and patronage. Through the decades it remained true to the call. The U.S. Supreme Court's 1990 *Rutan* decision effectively illegalized some of these peculiar old ways. What happened when *Rutan* met the Pennsylvania turnpike is a classic story of an irresistible force hitting the immovable object. We disappear down a black hole of outrageous reality, funny things happen, laws bend and break, and we risk finding ourselves in a Twilight Zone of untruths and obscuration.

The most enlightening aspect of the story is the remarkable cooperation displayed by politicians of both parties to break the law. The most interesting part of the story, I'd come to see, was that the two political parties display remarkable cooperation when it comes to doling out influence and receiving money for themselves. This private cooperation between the parties is the hidden politics seldom seen by the public. We usually only get to see the parties squabbling endlessly over public business. Budgets fail to pass, homelessness and alienation rise, schools and libraries decay, we the people in short go to hell before we get ours, but the two parties never fail to help each other get theirs.

Managers at the turnpike at first took the *Rutan* decision seriously. So much so that procedures were completely changed. To comply with the spirit as well as the letter of the law, the turnpike began to hold lotteries to fill vacancies. If you applied for a fare collection job your application wouldn't be decided by a politician. There was an honest-to-God fare collection lottery. Cardboard boxes were set out, one for each turnpike district, and the applications were sorted into the appropriate box. Luck of the draw won the fortunate applicant a job. Politics were out of the loop.

This direct attack on nearly two centuries of patronage proved too much for the politicians to stomach. The lottery system lasted only several months before it was by-and-large quashed. There's still an occasional lottery. But not often. Political pressure exerted from many quarters returned the turnpike to the old ways. Leaders in this assault, I'm told, were Republican state senator Jubelirer, and Democratic state senator (and former Philadelphia patronage boss) Fumo, and of course their willing political handmaidens, the commissioners of both parties. One commissioner at an executive session was heard to bellow, "I'm here to get what I can from this place!" Fumo, Jubelirer and the commissioners certainly were not alone, as everybody still badly wanted a thumb in the patronage pie.

The turnpike commissioners will tell you they try to comply with the *Rutan* decision. They'll say they hired an attorney, Peter Ennis, to write guidelines for the personnel committee. They'll tell you the personnel committee adopted this written policy. They'll tell you the personnel committee must advertise jobs, and must select candidates from a pool of at least three names. Though the committee may still accept letters of recommendation from politicians, I'm told those letters are affixed with a warning that the U.S. Supreme Court has ruled patronage hirings illegal.

Peter Ennis told me he'd been contracted by the turnpike to work on *Rutan* matters. He sounded friendly and open. He said he believed the turnpike began his contract about six months after the *Rutan* decision was handed down. Citing attorney/client privilege, he declined to talk about specifics. In general, he said, *Rutan* requires that government not take party interests into account when hiring or promoting. While it was true, he said, that the court allowed high-level, "vital interest" political appointments to continue, he said no jobs at the turnpike fell into this category. How had he landed his job? I asked. Through somebody in his firm, he told me.

John Hook, who retired as the turnpike's head of fare collection in December 1991, says he personally witnessed the new, "patronage-free" system work. He said once he sat in on a personnel committee meeting that recommended an unsponsored prospect for a job. A competitor who had political backing lost out, he said.

Most others told me the system doesn't work. Ennis, the attorney appointed to write the anti-patronage guidelines, is himself seen as a political appointment, viewed as having been selected by commissioner Malone as a favor to former attorney general Zimmerman, who now works in the same firm as Ennis. Ennis, despite his best intentions, may not even know his guidelines aren't always followed, I'm told. For example, jobs aren't always advertised, and there aren't always three applicants. One employee complained to me that the job of a recent turnpike hire wasn't advertised.

Even when there are three names, the system can be rigged. One old-timer remembered that governor Dick Thornburgh used to ask party bosses to submit applications with four other applications for a state job. The four "smoke screen" applications wouldn't even be considered.

The politics behind the personnel committee furthermore cast doubts on the sincerity of the process. The personnel committee was balanced between various factions in what some describe as an "eleven-way" division. Fumo, Jubelirer, the majority and minority in the house, and the governor are said to be among those controlling the committee.

"The turnpike's personnel committee works with seven members," one employee told me. "Three are allegedly neutral. They include the chief engineer, the executive director, and the head of human resources. The other four represent one of the politically appointed commissioners. Walter Lawson, the director of purchasing and brother-in-law of outgoing commissioner Ursomarso, represented his close relative. (Editor's note — Larsen, we're told, was replaced by senator Jubelirer's representative, Deborah Kovel.) Mr. Carnabuci, the assistant executive director for the western region and Republican patronage boss, represents commissioner Malone. Mr. Palermo, the associate executive director, represents commissioner Dodaro (and senator Fumo), while Mr. Shelton, the assistant executive director for the east and Democratic patronage boss, represents commissioner Brady. This is obviously a political committee and its run-around of the 1990 U.S. Supreme Court ruling against political patronage is astounding." Lawson (hired in February '92), Kovel (hired in October '91),

Palermo (promoted in August '91) and Shelton (promoted in August '91) themselves were all hired or promoted in violation of *Rutan*. Executive director Sokol hired his brother as geologist. How sensitive to the law can they be?

The politicians, who control the commissioners and the personnel committee, make the decisions about the jobs. So girlfriends and husbands and brothers and brothers-in-law still are hired. The committee's lawyer is seen as employed to make the case that the girlfriends and husbands and brothers and brothers-in-law, out of millions of Pennsylvanians, happen to be the most qualified holders of the jobs.

How does the system work? In March 1993, while conducting interviews for this book, I visited a legislative aide in Harrisburg. Without mentioning I had knowledge of the *Rutan* decision, I asked this aide how one goes about getting a job on the turnpike. He tells me the commissioners dole out the jobs, at the request of prominent politicians. Talk turned to Deborah Kovel, the assistant fare collection chief and friend of state senator Jubelirer. Kovel was hired in October 1991, herself a *Rutan* violation. Part of her job is to hire others. "She does a great job," he told me. "Some people complain that she's Jubelirer's girlfriend — I mean his friend — but she does a great job." At that moment the phone rang, and the aide, speaking into the phone, said this was a coincidence, that he'd just been talking about her and turnpike jobs. From where I sat I could hear a woman on the other end of the line. He thanked her for returning his call. While I sat and listened, my host tried to get a friend a turnpike job. He had an application for a summer toll taker's position in front of him and, as he fingered the application, the aide told his connection at the turnpike that his friend was qualified, with a college degree. His state representative, he told her, was passing the application along to the speaker of the house, who would give it to the commissioners with other applications. He complained over the phone that the present speaker of the house might not be around long, that whatever happened he hoped his friend would get a job and would appreciate whatever help he could get.

My host hung up and smiled at me and said, "See, that's how it works."

"So you give your applications to the speaker of the house, who gets the commissioners to make the hire?" I asked.

"That's right." He explained the process was presently hampered by uncertainties, as the leadership of the house was perhaps up for grabs. "In the old days, when (late representative James) Manderino was house speaker, he was powerful and you knew where you stood." These days, when trying to get jobs for pals, he explained, one would be well advised to go through other politicians than the house speaker. "You go wherever the power is," he explained.

We still hadn't had time to get down to the subject of my visit. He'd been too busy trying to impress me with his influence.

"What about the 1990 *Rutan* decision, making all this illegal?" I asked.

The aide seemed to start in his chair. "Well, yes," he spat. "These days all hiring at the turnpike is done through the personnel committee. They rotate the members and they're very careful about obeying the law. It's all very strict and in accordance with the law. They review all applications and they're very careful to keep politics out of it."

He completely countermanded everything he'd just told me, and everything I'd just witnessed.

You hear it high, you hear it low. In Pennsylvania, years after the *Rutan* decision, the way to get in isn't to fill out an application at the Job Service. I interviewed one turnpike maintenance employee who told me she got her job in the spring of 1992 thanks to the help of a relation, who was a turnpike secretary, and associate executive director Michael Palermo. "Let's face it," she told me, "this is how you get a job. There must be a hundred applicants for every job and you need help from someone on the inside." She said turnpike jobs are advertised on a bulletin board but, in the end, you need the help of someone on the inside to land the job. "Let's face it," she repeated, "that's how you get a job anywhere." I asked if she realized patronage hiring was now illegal. She gave me a funny look, as if she did not understand the language I was speaking, or the planet I was from. No, she said, that didn't make sense. Everybody knows, she said, you need help on the inside to get a job.

Other political manipulations by the commissioners and the committees they control foster further distrust.

For example, commissioner Ursomarso in 1991 requested that a turnpike computer terminal be installed in his Delaware car dealership. Dozens of people attending the computer systems committee meeting raised no objection. Ursomarso had no business installing a state terminal off commonwealth premises, everyone seems to agree. Let alone installing it in Delaware. Why hadn't anyone on the oversight committee, charged with security, objected?

Then there are the jobs the commissioners are said to control in private industry. The overreach of the commissioners is seen as extending into the private businesses of outside contractors.

One commissioner's son is said to have a job with a friendly insurance counsel; the insurance counsel also sells fundraising tickets for the commissioner. Another employee complained that an engineering consulting firm hired a relative of one of the commissioners to serve as a subconsultant for public relations on a turnpike project.

The sway of the commissioners and the politicians over the contractors can be understood when one considers, for example, the make-up of the turnpike's engineer consultant selection committee. Like the personnel committee, its majority is seen as composed of political operatives, including John Boschi, the deputy executive director of maintenance. Why is the turnpike's head of maintenance helping to select highway engineers? I was asked. (One turnpike executive defended Boschi's place on the engineer selection committee, telling me Boschi's maintenance oversight did in fact mesh with engineer selection.)

Dishonesty has become so institutionalized in Pennsylvania that everyone seems to be in an amazing and continuous state of denial.

Funny, ironic stories arise out of all this deception and delusion. These stories also attest to the inefficiency of patronage. *Rutan* was violated in August 1991, when Republican commissioner Ursomarso's brother-in-law, Walter Lawson, got a $26 dollar-an-hour job as a turnpike special assistant in the eastern region. It was violated again when Lawson was promoted director of purchasing at $30 an hour. Lawson, a former salesman of Saab automobiles, had no purchasing experience, his co-workers complain. The department quickly fell behind. Backed-up purchase orders soon rose into piles, employees say, several feet high. I started hearing stories about the piles of purchase orders, stories of people who'd try to stick their order ahead of others'. Part-timers were brought in. Bill Cornelius was a former director of purchasing who received early retirement incentives under what's called the Mellow Window, after its sponsor, state senator Robert Mellow. Cornelius returned to the turnpike on a part-time basis to help straighten things out. (A sixteen-year veteran of the turnpike, Cornelius confirmed all this. He said he thought restrictions in patronage hirings might prove impossible to enforce.)

Jeff Hess, son of state representative Dick Hess, was promoted to assistant director of purchasing at a salary of $25 an hour, or $52,000 a year, on February 21, 1992. "He, like the others, has little experience with purchasing. The purchasing department is a real mess," one employee told me. Jeff Hess started with the turnpike in 1985 as a field auditor at a salary of $902 biweekly. He lives in Bedford, "in the same area as two other Hess's with the turnpike commission," I was told.

In late 1992, purchasing director Larsen hired James Weikert as a procurement officer. Weikert's wife, Brenda, turnpike employees complain, is a member of senator Jubelirer's staff.

At least he has company. Brian Swett, hired on February 18, 1992, as a technical analyst within fare collection, is married to Susan Swett, secretary to senator Fumo. Mr. Swett replaced someone who left under the retirement incentive measure. "Several well-qualified persons within the turnpike applied for Swett's job, but were rejected," one co-worker complained. Swett's salary for this appointment was set at $1,423.20 biweekly.

As humorous as these stories are, they are often tinged with sadness. One employee told me of the sad experience of witnessing an unsuspecting applicant hopefully apply for a job when the employee knew the opening was pre-slated to go to an insider.

One employee complained to me, for example, that in November 1992, the husband of director Sokol's secretary was hired as an operations review analyst.

Another employee complained that a friend of state police captain Russell Clanagan was hired in 1992 as a secretary. Work backed up, and a temp was hired to help Clanagan's friend fight the backlog. Someone found out the temp lived in a campground. (This story reminds me of the days in the 1930s when turnpike construction workers and their families lived in tents.) The top executive staff was so shocked to learn that the temp was living in a campground that they chipped in to give her a security deposit for an apartment, and gave her permanent work.

Employees joke about which families have the most members on the payroll. One secretary enjoys the company of two sisters, a brother and a brother-in-law. Employee rolls glitter with similar surnames. Brandee, Jeffry, Natalie, Jay and John Bortz. Christina and Dewayne Hampton. Clare, Leigh and Heather Doran. Jeffrey, Kenneth and Donald Hess. John, Maria and Andrea Kohler. Barbara, James and Daunette Pecora. Mark and Michael Ecker. James and Jacqueline DeMarco. Joseph and Deborah Kovel. S. Michael, Frank and Daniel Palermo. Thomas, John and Jennifer Sokol.

The turnpike's employment records to this day list the "relation at PTC (Pennsylvania Turnpike Commission)" and "relationship" of one employee to another. Jacqueline DeMarco's employment record, for example, lists one Michael Kessler as her "relation at PTC," and his relationship to her as "uncle." (These spaces are often left blank in cases of a relation to a director or a commissioner.)

Most all these nepotistic hires and promotions were for low- to middle-level jobs. Certainly covered by *Rutan* restrictions. Some of these relatives held jobs long before *Rutan,* illustrating a strong historical inertia against reform. Many were hired or promoted months or years after *Rutan.*

Sometimes these hires or promotions are opposed. The joke among employees is that associate executive director Mike Palermo has the most relatives on the dole. The story goes that Palermo wanted someone promoted out of a toll collector's job. John Hook, then deputy executive director for fare collection, opposed the promotion.

There is an ongoing problem with dishonest toll collectors pocketing money and toll tickets. You pocket a few toll tickets, add up the tolls, then pocket the money. The honesty of toll collectors is tested by undercover state troopers who drive up to a booth and present a marked toll ticket with payment. At the end of the day, if a marked ticket isn't turned in by the collector, the cops have an idea money has been pocketed. At the end of 1992 nineteen toll takers were arrested.

District justices got sick of handling what they considered to be a never-ending stream of small-time toll collection robberies. They decreed that the cops would have to prove at least five marked tickets had disappeared before a toll collector could be prosecuted. Not wanting to promote Palermo's choice, the story goes, Hook audited the toll collector and discovered two marked tickets had been reported missing from his booth. It wasn't enough to prosecute the collector, but it was enough to keep him from a promotion.

John Hook, now retired from his job as deputy executive director of fare collection, spent thirty-one years at the turnpike, starting as a clerk, working his way up. He spoke to me from his bed, recovering from surgery. He has many happy memories of the turnpike. He lives in Mount Carmel, and described himself as a politician, with a politician's point of view, as he holds a seat on town council. His turnpike job no longer on the line, he spoke, for the most part, with refreshing candor.

He agrees he had his tussles with Mike Palermo and others over hirings and promotions, but he played all that down. If he was asked to promote a fare collector, and the auditors found missing or stolen fares, he says he'd simply tell the sponsor, "Let's sit on that guy a while."

"What's going on today isn't what I call patronage," he says. "What patronage means to me is how it was thirty years ago, when I started on the turnpike: One party comes in and everyone's fired."

The Pennsylvania governor's office in the early 1960s controlled more than 70,000 jobs. One of the biggest hits to state patronage came on July 23, 1970, with the passage of Act 195, which authorized union negotiations and strikes. The American Federation of State, County and Municipal Employees soon demanded civil service protection for 68,000 state and local employees. The governor's office still controlled 24,000 state patronage employees by the time Act 195 was signed. The next governor to take office, Milton Shapp, controlled only 4,000 jobs. By the time governor Robert Casey came to office in 1987 the number had dropped many hundred lower. Patronage was not what it used to be.

In the 1960s, Hook remembered, employees regularly received computer printouts demanding $50 "contributions" to whichever party was in power. He said the first time he received a printout he refused to cooperate. "I was called upstairs," he says. "I told them I wasn't going to give them $50. The girl told me 'Have the $50 turned in tomorrow or don't come into work Friday.'" He says that night he went and told his county chairman about it. "So the chairman took $50 out of his pocket and threw it at me. He said, 'Anybody who'd lose his job over $50 is stupid.'" He says he returned the money to the chairman, then "contributed" his own $50. After that they wanted $50 from him twice a year.

"You wouldn't believe how dramatically things have changed since those days," he says. Mostly, he says, things changed with the growth of unions in the 1970s, and particularly because employees began taking the turnpike to court, where they won lawsuits. The suits were effective, he says. Patronage firings stopped.

As for awarding public jobs to friends and relatives, Hook says, "That'll never end, that'll never stop." Why not? I ask. "Speaking as a politician myself," he explains, "it's always good to award jobs. If you can award jobs you figure those people can help you get votes."

During his ten or eleven years as director of fare collection, he says, he was "always" contacted by legislators, and others, for jobs. He says the *Rutan* decision was a bad one. "It's unrealistic," he told me. "I know what you call patronage hiring is against the law. The commissioners know it's against the law. That's why they hired an outside lawyer to make guidelines. But of course it's never going to work."

Lotteries are unworkable, he says. Lotteries hire idiots who have the luck of the draw. The best way to hire someone, he says, is through referral. "It happens in every business, no matter what the law says. I don't understand that law."

Even so, he told me, when he left the turnpike in late '91 the commissioners were "making a sincere effort to comply. That's why they began the lotteries, and hired the outside lawyer to make the guidelines for the personnel committee."

He sounded surprised to hear that the lotteries, for the most part, were no longer conducted.

I asked how it came to pass that Deborah Kovel, the deputy assistant for fare collection, had been hired as his deputy in October 1991. (In fact, turnpike employees say, Kovel's patron, senator Jubelirer, pushed her for the head job in fare collection, to succeed Hook. A *political fight* broke out over her appointment, with the four appointed commissioners stalemated along party lines; a compromise was reached and she was finally given the assistant's job. Low-level employment decisions are not supposed to be subject to political fights.) Hook at first said he wouldn't comment on Kovel for the record, only that she had been "brought in" for him to train before he retired. Then, as he got wound up about how much he disliked the *Rutan* decision, he blurted, "Why should that person, because she's (senator) Jubelirer's girlfriend, be eliminated from a job?" He was making a fascinating discrimination argument, the crux of which was that not to dole out jobs to party hacks, friends, lovers and cronies was to discriminate against the poor devils.

Why should public hiring be any different from business hiring? he asked. I'd come to hear this question with stunning regularity. I replied that government, unlike a business, belonged to *all* the people, that everyone deserved a fair shot, not just well placed clans. He didn't argue, but told me he longed for the good old days.

One exasperated turnpike employee, summing up the ingrained milieu of dishonest hirings and promotions, told me, "Everything they do, in my mind, is illegal." With a hint of sadness this person said, "The shame of it is, it didn't have to be this way. The turnpike makes lots of money and is semi-independent. It could really have been something if the politicians had only left it alone."

7

The Secret, Well-Mannered Minuet

These *Rutan* violations certainly are illegal and outrageous, but perhaps most outrageous are the practices at the turnpike and throughout government that remain legal. We've seen that the hiring procedures are cozy and incestuous, creating inefficiency, waste, and special treatment. Now consider the legalized system of kickbacks and bribery loosely called "pinstripe patronage."

Contractors, legal counsel and bond underwriters are soaking taxpayers for millions of dollars, then kicking back millions of dollars in profits to politicians. In Pennsylvania this inbred system of legalized contractor corruption has begun to generate questions about the very independence, integrity and fairness of our government and our justice system.

Several employees complained that turnpike associate executive director S. Michael Palermo used his influence to have the commission purchase its new eastern regional headquarters from his former real estate associate, Joseph Tarantino of Norristown's Continental Realty. "Palermo said it was okay, since his own real estate license is in escrow," one employee told me. Records indicate the turnpike bought the building for $2,150,000 on December 3, 1991.

The new regional headquarters sits beside mile marker 330.2 of the turnpike, at 251 Flint Hill Road in King of Prussia. A large, modern office building, it has its own ramp onto the turnpike. I visited the new building over Thanksgiving 1992, while it was still unoccupied. I walked around the expansive grounds, taking in the running paths and outdoor handball courts.

I telephoned the old eastern regional headquarters, at the time still open for business, and asked the receptionist for the name of the broker who had sold the turnpike its new building. "Joe Tarantino, of Continental in Norristown," she answered in a flash. This was just the switchboard operator.

Records at the state bureau of professional and occupational affairs list an S. Michael Palermo as holding an associate real estate broker's license that has been inactive since 1990. At the time his real estate license lapsed in 1990 he was listed as working with Continental Realty of Norristown. He first registered to sell real estate on April 1, 1975, according to state records. Palermo has been with the turnpike since 1985. He is usually described by his co-workers as enjoying the long-time friendship and patronage of state senator Fumo. In September 1985, Palermo became the turnpike's eastern region assistant executive director, or the Democratic patronage boss, a position he held until *August 20, 1991,* when he was promoted to associate executive director. (Patronage promotions, you'll recall, were ruled unconstitutional by the Supreme Court's *Rutan* decision in June, 1990.)

Tarantino's real estate license dates back to December 14, 1973, according to state records. One turnpike worker remembered that Tarantino used to work on the turnpike, in maintenance, I was told. After Tarantino left the turnpike to concentrate on real estate he paved over a surplus piece of turnpike property to serve as his parking lot. The turnpike sent a standard letter asking him to vacate its property. Tarantino's state representative then contracted the turnpike, requesting that the realtor be allowed to rent the parcel. The turnpike complied. Tarantino's rent on the parcel, strangely, began to decrease over the years, I was told.

It was Mike Palermo's suggestion that the turnpike buy the building offered by Tarantino. Palermo drafted a memorandum justifying the purchase. His memo reviewed four possibilities for the new eastern regional headquarters, including the Flint Hill Road property. Palermo's memo ended with the recommendation that the turnpike buy the building offered by his former real estate firm. Turnpike officials were "scared" by the conflict, and instructed Palermo to have no more to do with the sale. Palermo distanced himself. Shortly thereafter, the commission made an offer for the building.

Records in the Montgomery County Recorder of Deeds office

describe the new regional headquarters as a 37,925 square foot multi-office building constructed in 1977 on 4.39 acres of land. The property was deeded to a Robert DiMarco on January 20, 1986, for one dollar. On September 16, 1986, DiMarco sold the property to Flint Hill Road Associates for $975,000. In 1991, at the time of sale to the turnpike, the realty transfer tax statement of value set its fair market value at $1,424,120.

At least one turnpike employee expressed an official opinion that the turnpike could have paid less than $2,150,000. The building originally listed for about $3.2 million, I was told. The turnpike representative handling the negotiations first offered $1.4 million, close to the fair market value. The owners then reduced the price to $2.8 million. The turnpike's representative informed the commission that the depressed 1991 real estate market was soft, and recommended holding out for a price well below $2 million. The negotiator was overruled. "The commissioners seemed to want the building at any price," I was told.

One employee expressed the opinion that the agency prevented its representative from driving a harder bargain. How can we fairly judge whether the turnpike overpaid for the building? I was asked. Palermo and Tarantino seem satisfied. Who can say whether the public got the best agreement?

Turnpike employees say Tarantino's commission for the sale was in the six figures, though I'm told he recently surrendered some of the commission due to problems with the building's roof. Tarantino also holds a consulting contract with the turnpike, for work connected with the old Reading/Lancaster interchange. That's not all. In 1993 Tarantino serves as the turnpike's "land use consultant." "There's a turnpike Land Use Committee," I was told. "Joe Tarantino submitted a bid to become the committee's consultant. His bid turned out to be the lowest. Now Wal-Mart wants to buy some land from the turnpike and Tarantino's the negotiator." I attempted to contact Tarantino, but he did not respond.

The Republicans didn't object to the eastern regional office deal, one employee explained, because in another year or so it will be their turn to award the turnpike's new western regional office.

No one kicks, because everybody seems to have their own hustle going. The commissioners and the politicians all have their own sweetheart contractors. One commissioner, for example, has a favored contractor in Belle Vernon, a worked complained. At the Pennsylvania turnpike you encounter endless stories of sweetheart deals and occasional screw-ups. My favorite story? A few years ago, an engineering firm in Westmoreland County built a bridge underpass that was too low.

Members of both parties display a bottomless well of cooperation while they pass out lucrative contracts to each other's friends. Consider the selection of attorneys who represent the turnpike commission. When people sue the turnpike, the commission contacts the state attorney general's office to ask if the AG wishes to represent the agency in court. This has really become no more than a courtesy, as the attorney general's office seldom performs the work. (The governor of Pennsylvania in 1993 requested a budget of $65 million for the attorney general's office, a $6 million increase over the previous year; the attorney general employs hundreds of in-house lawyers, all collecting high pay. The AG's office still has no resources or inclination to handle all the state's legal work — but that's another story.)

So the attorney general invariably delegates the task of representing the turnpike back to the commission. This causes the turnpike's legal department to send a memo to Republican commissioner Malone and Democratic commissioner Dodaro, advising them to select an outside attorney. There are no bids. The two parties graciously take turns selecting a favored law firm. The Democrats take a pick; next time, the Republicans get a pick.

Democrat Dodaro in 1992 often selected either the law firm of Saul, Ewing, Remick & Saul (which is the firm of then-house speaker Bob O'Donnell), or Astor, Weiss & Newman (which is the law firm of senator Fumo). These are sometimes large contracts. In late 1992, for example, Saul, Ewing, Remick & Saul billed the turnpike $64,640 for services rendered and expenses for a single complicated case. Among firms selected by Republican Malone was Rawle & Henderson, of Philadelphia, founded in 1783 as the Rawle Law

Office, and recognized as the oldest continuing practice in the United States. Not all selections were so venerable. It was presumably Dodaro who selected Stephen Zappala, Jr., son of the state supreme court justice, to perform a small amount of turnpike legal work. ("Steve, Jr., hasn't really done much work for the turnpike," I'm told. "He handled a small case involving a truck that hit a turnpike bridge.")

We should all take heart by this high level of cooperation. The Democrats pick a lawyer. Next time, the Republicans get one. I've come to see this patronage dance as an intricate, genteel, well-mannered minuet. In matters of their own business, the two parties never miss their turn, their bow, the cooperative wink.

Just try to pass a budget, fund a library, feed kids at school, buy books, make our tax system more fair, rebuild our cities, provide opportunities for our young people — in short, all the things that make our society work — there the inter-party cooperation ends.

While I was writing this book, in December 1992, state house speaker Bob O'Donnell was deposed, replaced as speaker by William DeWeese of Green County. O'Donnell's law firm, since his replacement, hasn't received turnpike legal work, I'm told. Soon after DeWeese's elevation to speaker the turnpike did however select a Green County bank to hold a $35 million liquid fuel tax deposit.

8

Unholy Pinstripe Patronage

The Pennsylvania Turnpike Commission, by purchasing its two million dollar eastern headquarters through a director's former real estate associate, had committed one of the greatest sins a government body can perpetrate. The commission was spending insensitively and lavishly in a time of recession. The government, unlike you and me, never runs out of money. Even so it must remain sensitive to the times. Otherwise you display that you are out of touch with the public. You are like those permanent guests in Jay Gatsby's mansion, staying long after the party is over.

What caused such a disconnection with the public at the turnpike? Didn't this disregard for public sentiment (and the law, in the case of *Rutan* violations) signal an insular, clubby attitude? How had this attitude come about? Could this elitism rear its blow-dried head in other areas, perhaps betraying deeper problems within our state government? These were some of the thoughts that began to enter my mind.

At the Pennsylvania turnpike, all sign posts of trouble point to its practice of underwriting bonds, and its attendant bond counseling. In recent years the turnpike has floated almost a billion and a half dollars worth of bonds, generating huge commissions. Bond underwriting is by far and away the biggest service contracted by the turnpike (and, increasingly, other government agencies). It sets the tone for every smaller deal down the line.

Didn't I realize how much these bond underwriters were making? one turnpike employee after another asked me. One explained it bluntly. There was in 1992 a $570 *million* turnpike bond issue. Did I realize that for every $1,000 in bonds, the underwriter receives a commission of about $3.75? The profits of the bond counselors aren't far behind. The profits are enormous, running, some years, into the millions. The politicians select the underwriters and the counselors on a no-bid basis, much the same as the commissioners select turnpike attorneys without seeing a bid. The favored bond underwriters and counselors, in turn, give hundreds of thousands of dollars in legalized kickbacks to the politicians.

This clubby arrangement is certainly good for the bond underwriters and the politicians. How good is it for the state as a whole, its institutions, and its people? The rarefied air of bond underwriting carries more than a putrid whiff of privilege. To what extent, I wondered, does the corrupted atmosphere filter into other areas of government? Was our justice system, for instance, at all perverted by this quaint system of legalized kickbacks?

In Pennsylvania, because the turnpike's chief bond underwriter happens to be the brother of a state supreme court justice, this question is of growing import and interest.

The practice of awarding no-bid contracts in Pennsylvania came to articulated fruition during the governorship of Republican lawyer Richard Thornburgh.

Contracts certainly were awarded on a political basis throughout the history of the commonwealth. Precedent, as the U.S. Supreme Court reminds us in the *Rutan* decision, doesn't make right. Often the awarding of state contracts was quite brazenly political, and certainly questionable. M. Harvey Taylor, an insurance agent who happened to be the Republican president pro tempore of the state senate in the 1950s and into the 60s, used to handle much of the state's insurance business. (When old-timers ran into trouble with the law or the state a marvelous and popular euphemism was, "I guess it's time to go down and buy some insurance from Harve.")

Governor Thornburgh unapologetically exacerbated our problem with no-bid contractors. Thornburgh boasted of a scheme to reduce the state's payroll by tens of thousands of public employees. What he didn't trumpet so loudly was that much of the work that previously had been performed by state employees — from snow removal to legal work — now had to be performed by outside contractors. Often Thornburgh awarded these contracts as political favors, on a no-bid basis. These contractors became big contributors to political campaigns, including Thornburgh's.

Thornburgh awarded millions of dollars in no-bid legal work. This later became a campaign issue. State treasurer R. Budd Dwyer, on the day he shot himself to death in his office, charged that Thornburgh had been obliged to dump great sums into attorney general LeRoy Zimmerman's 1984 re-election campaign. Zimmerman's opponent, Allen Ertel, if elected, planned to investigate Thornburgh for awarding the no-bid contracts and receiving the resulting political kickbacks, the treasurer charged. Zimmerman was barely re-elected, and was dogged with charges of corruption throughout his second term.

Bad government leads to more bad government. The corrupting practice of awarding no-bid contracts in the early 1980s laid the groundwork for the biggest no-bid money grab in state history — a 1986 Pennsylvania turnpike bond issue for $807 million.

Throughout the eight years of the Republican Thornburgh administration the Democrats had been shut out of the awarding of contracts. They retaliated by causing gridlock wherever possible. A continuous battle ensued for control of the turnpike commission and its plums. There have traditionally been two turnpike commissioners from each party. The governor formally names each appointment, which must be approved by two thirds of the state senate. So he must take the counsel of the senators. If he doesn't, it means trouble. Various factions would often shoot down even their own party members if that nomination seemed unable to provide proper largesse.

The fight was really about gaining control of awarding the lucrative bond work, and the resulting political contributions. To get his nominee Frank Ursomarso onto the commission in 1984, Thornburgh was forced to accept James Dodaro as Democratic commissioner. So Republican Thornburgh's greed set the stage for the monumental greed shown by the Democrats over the next decade.

In 1985, wanting to end the gridlock at the turnpike and proceed with various highway expansion projects (and to get those contributions rolling in), Thornburgh cut an infamous deal with late house majority leader, and Democrat, James Manderino. Known officially as Act 61 (signed September 30, 1985), the legislation authorized $4 billion in turnpike projects. Thornburgh and Manderino agreed that each job associated with the turnpike bond issue would be performed by two firms, one from each party. They called it the "Noah's Ark Deal." The idea, as with Noah's Ark, was that "everybody would come along." Everybody, that is, but outsiders.

The size of the proposed bond issue, the prospect of awarding the bond work on a no-bid basis, and the opportunity for the resulting political contributions caused the two parties to happily strike the Noah's Ark deal. At the time the transaction was estimated to be worth more than $10 million in fees to the associated brokerage houses. One turnpike observer shared the opinion that total profits were actually much higher. The deal was composed of short- and long-term bonds. The short-term bonds would periodically be refinanced or "remarketed." The numerous remarketings of short term bonds, one observer estimated, nets the bondsellers $5 million in fees each time. The financial firms argue that the fees are offset by lower interest rates, which compensates the state. Who knows? "The interest rates and the amortizations on these deals are so complicated," one interested party told me, "you have to be Einstein to figure it out."

All told, the profits of the long-term bond issue, the refinancing of the short-term bonds, the legal work, and proceeds to all the associated, smaller brokers down the line, might in the end have created fees approaching $100 million, I was told. Nice work, if you can get it. No one's ever conducted an official tally of profits from the 1986 deal. One thing's certain: it was by far and away the largest bond float ever conducted by the commonwealth of Pennsylvania. (The next largest Pennsylvania bond issue, according to the industry publication The Bond Buyer, was a $375 million float in 1950 for veteran's assistance.)

Before 1986, the awarding of bond issues wasn't the cut-and-dried, turn-it-over-to-our-sweethearts proposition that it has lately become. In comparison, the last turnpike bond offering in the late 1970s, for climbing lanes, amounted to only about $75 million, I was told. That bond issue wasn't a no-bid giveaway. Requests were made to the bonding community for proposals.

The 1986 bond issue was not only monumentally large. Of greater significance, the rules of the game were changed to award mind-boggling sums of no-bid work. This financed equally staggering campaign contributions from the grateful, inside-crowd bond dealers. The politicians, and their buddy bond brokers, cashed in big.

The rumblings over the huge and impending 1986 bond issue sent seismic tremors through the American investment community. "There was no doubt for two or three years there was going to be a transaction by the Pennsylvania Turnpike Commission," Charles Gomulka, a partner in the investment firm of Russell Rea & Zappala told the Pittsburgh Post-Gazette in a 1986 article. "Firms began talking to commissioners and legislators to make their capabilities known."

Republican commissioner James Malone told the Post-Gazette, "I had a stack of booklets (from financial firms) three or four feet high. I read enough to know there was no way I could distinguish one from the other."

That's because there is no real difference between the bond firms. The deciding factor would center around which firms the politicians trusted to kick back the proceeds. Again we see both parties gleefully cooperating when it means cash in their tills. They compromised to allow the bond issue to proceed. The compromise included temporarily increasing the size of the turnpike commission from four to six members — three for each party. The spare Democratic commissioner had been selected after consultations with Manderino, Fumo, and state senate Democratic leader Edward Zemprelli, of Clairton.

In the end they awarded the contracts in a private session on May 27, 1986. The process resembled a pick-up ball game. The six commissioners took turns naming their picks for senior underwriters, co-managers and counsels. The plum award for the Democrats, that of senior underwriter, went to Russell, Rea & Zappala, of Pittsburgh. It would receive an estimated $1.5 million in revenue from the selection.

By this time Stephen Zappala had been a state supreme court justice for more than three years, having won election in 1982. Zappala's family has been involved in Pennsylvania politics for decades. Justice Zappala's father, Frank, was a Pittsburgh magistrate and state legislator. Frank Zappala had four sons, all lawyers. Two sons, Richard and Frank, went on to become real estate developers. Charles became an investment banker. Stephen attended Notre Dame, Pittsburgh's Duquesne University, then Georgetown Law School. He was solicitor for the Allegheny County Community College in 1974, then served as solicitor for Allegheny County from 1974 to 1976. He was elected to common pleas court in 1979. From there he successfully stood for election to the state supreme court. One of his early supporters for supreme court was state senator Fumo.

Employees at the turnpike talk endlessly about the long-time, mentor's relationship bestowed by justice Stephen Zappala upon his protégé, commissioner Dodaro. Dodaro has known the justice and his family since his childhood. The justice's father, Frank, sponsored Dodaro through Duquesne University Law School. Stephen Zappala and Dodaro later became law partners. (Dodaro's biography in the Pennsylvania Manual lists him as a member of the law firm Zappala, Dodaro & Cambest from 1970 to 1979.) Dodaro's footsteps always seem not far behind Stephen Zappala. Dodaro, following his mentor, served as solicitor for the Allegheny County Community College in 1985. The state manual lists him as "solicitor, Allegheny Co. Dept., of Law, 1985." Justice Stephen Zappala then used his influence to advocate that Dodaro be named a commissioner on the turnpike. In 1984, duly nominated by Thornburgh, Dodaro took his place at the turnpike.

When it came time to award the no-bid bonds in 1986, Dodaro was there to help his old childhood friends, the Zappalas. Fellow Democratic commissioner James Goodman, the Democrat's temporary pick for the commission, remembers Dodaro unabashedly pushing for the selection of Russell, Rea & Zappala, of Pittsburgh, as senior underwriter for the '86 deal. Charles Zappala, principal in the firm, was the brother to Dodaro's patron, the supreme court justice.

By most accounts the investment firm of Russell, Rea & Zappala was skillful at landing work, and performing work. In the early days the firm made use of sports personalities to woo potential business in sports-mad Pittsburgh. Former Pittsburgh Steelers fullback Robert "Rocky" Blier, for one example, once a partner in the firm, signed footballs at city council meetings to help land bond work. The question of the moment is whether Russell, Rea & Zappala became *too* skilled at landing work.

James Goodman served as the temporary Democratic turnpike commissioner from September 1985 to June 1987. Now he's with the state liquor control board. Manderino put him on the turnpike commission, Goodman told me.

"It was clear that Dodaro was pushing for Russell, Rea & Zappala to serve as senior underwriter," Goodman remembers. He said it appeared to him that Dodaro supported RR&Z even before Goodman began his term in late 1985. I asked Goodman if there were any concerns of possible conflicts since Dodaro had been Stephen Zappala's law partner. He expressed surprise to learn that the two had been in practice together. He said he knew both had been Allegheny County solicitors, but until I'd told him he hadn't known they'd shared a law practice. "That would have undoubtedly concerned me," he said. "It would have allowed me to pause."

He genuinely seemed surprised and a little bit troubled. "Did they both have their names in the name of the firm?" he asked. They did, I told him. Goodman explained he hailed "clear from the other end of the state." Pittsburghers, he said, must have known the two were partners. He said it was easy to sit in judgment seven years down the road. Had he known at the time Dodaro and Steve Zappala had been partners, he said, he may have still supported RR&Z as the senior underwriter. The point was, he said, a manager has to be concerned when he or she is involved in a decision that may contain a possible conflict of interest.

Following the '86 bond issue, RR&Z "became a major player," he observed, "a senior underwriter with Merrill, Lynch. It made them."

Goodman recalled the selection of RR&Z was only one of many inside deals in the '86 bond deal. The factional, political nature of the commission, and the complexity of bond underwriting, it seemed to him, all but guaranteed political selection of the bonding agents. He said a CEO in a private company would have an easier time awarding bond work by merit — or, at least, choosing the criteria by which merit could be weighed. Had he been asked by Manderino to award work to a favored underwriter? I asked. No, he replied. Manderino simply instructed him to help break the deadlock on the commission, which had been tied up for years. He recalled that Thornburgh for some time had been trying to fill the commission but his nominations kept getting shot down in the senate. Manderino's solution was to temporarily expand the commission to three votes for each party, making four votes the working majority.

Is there a better way to award bond work? I asked.

"To me it seems there should be a better way, but I don't know what it is," he replied.

"You don't have many firms in public finance that aren't politically connected," Dodaro told the Pittsburgh paper in 1986. "I make no bones that knowing someone is a plus (to the firms). We don't need to explain any of the firms because the entire team is made up of very capable, reputable firms with a Pennsylvania base."

Nevertheless, all seem to agree, the Dodaro/Zappala connection broke new ground for coziness. It was as if they didn't care, or had no perception, how this relationship might look to others. This callousness would come back to haunt them.

Thornburgh's aides, for their part, told reporters that supreme court justice Zappala had earlier played a "key role" in lobbying Thornburgh to appoint Dodaro to the turnpike commission. They nastily hinted the obvious: Stephen Zappala had put Dodaro on the turnpike commission, who had returned the favor by giving a million and a half worth of work to his patron's brother. Thornburgh left little high ground for himself. The Republicans selected Merrill, Lynch, Pierce, Fenner & Smith as their senior underwriter. In 1984 Merrill, Lynch had hired Thornburgh press secretary and advisor Paul Critchlow as vice president. Other lower-level Thornburgh aides found work with Critchlow.

Merrill, Lynch received the same estimated $1.5 million compensation as Russell, Rea & Zappala.

Defending themselves, RR&Z and commissioner Dodaro often point out that Russell, Rea & Zappala are deserving of turnpike bond work because RR&Z is a strong, Pennsylvania-based firm. Steven Dickson, who writes about underwriting for the industry daily The Bond Buyer, has another opinion. He told me RR&Z is only big and strong thanks to the work it received from Dodaro by way of the Pennsylvania turnpike. He points out that if you subtract the turnpike work, as the chart below suggests, RR&Z becomes a much smaller firm:

RR&Z's biggest clients 1988-92	Principal Amount	Number of Issues
Pennsylvania Turnpike Commission	$1,353	4
Allegheny Co. Residential Finance Authority	173	14
Erie Co. Prison Authority	130	1
Allegheny Co. Institution District	94	1
Westmoreland County	93	3

All dollars in millions   Source: The Bond Buyer & Securities Data Co.

Compare RR&Z with its principal competitors and you see that, without the insider turnpike work, its size would shrink appreciably:

Top underwriters of Pennsylvania Bonds 1992	Principal Amount	Number of issues	Market Share
Smith Barney, Harris Upham & Co.	$1,173	16	9.6%
Wheat First/Butcher & Singer	1,033	74	8.4
RRZ Public Markets	998	39	8.1
Merrill, Lynch & Co.	974	23	7.9
PNC Securities Corp.	924	66	7.5

All dollars in millions   Source: The Bond Buyer & Securities Data Co.

The 1986 bond issue put RR&Z right up there with Merrill, Lynch, as commissioner Goodman observed.

Industry writer Dickson seemed appalled at the way government conducts its bonding business. "The firm's competitors say they are resigned to the fact that RR&Z will lead-manage turnpike deals," Dickson wrote in the February 1, 1993 issue of The Bond Buyer, "but most said they do not believe the firm is doing anything wrong by nurturing personal relationships to garner business.

"'This is the currency of public finance work,' one Philadelphia source said," Dickson wrote.

Steven Dickson told me, with detectable amazement, that most of these investment houses truly seem to think all this is the best and only way to conduct public business. It's as if they never heard of competitive bids. "They just don't get it," he told me.

The 1986 selections of RR&Z and Merrill, Lynch as senior underwriters were not the only unholy alliances. Of most interest to us today is the Dodaro/Zappala connection, but in 1986 that big, wet smack on the cheek was just another romance at the orgy.

Even before the enabling legislation was signed, Republican commissioner Ursomarso, a White House aide in the Gerald Ford administration, had been approached by former president Ford himself, then a member of the board of directors of investment firm Shearson, Lehman Bros. Ford personally pitched Ursomarso on Shearson, Lehman. That firm ultimately was hired by the Republicans as a financial consultant, a deal estimated to have been worth at least $600,000.

The Democrats selected as co-manager, or bondseller, the Philadelphia office of Prudential-Bache, headed by Mark Schwartz. Schwartz had been an attorney with the state house Democrats, and a former aide to house speaker K. Leroy Irvis. Prudential-Bache stood to take in an estimated $700,000.

Republican commissioner Malone recommended Scheetz, Smith & Co., of Pittsburgh, as co-manager. A principal in that firm, Ted Scheetz, was an important contributor to the Republican party, and his company also handled Malone's personal investments. Scheetz, Smith & Co. stood to reap $500,000 in revenues from the bond issue.

For bond counsel, the Democrats selected the Pittsburgh firm Baskin, Flaherty, Elliott & Mannino. Partner James Flaherty, once an Allegheny County commissioner, was the brother of former Pittsburgh mayor and gubernatorial candidate Pete Flaherty.

Another Pittsburgh firm, Rose, Schmidt, Chapman, Duff & Hasley, won selection as Republican bond counsel. Partner Evans Rose served as finance chairman for Thornburgh's two runs for governor, and proceeded commissioner Malone as finance chairman of the state Republican party.

These and other companies saw estimated revenues totaling some $11 million from the 1986 bond issue. The turnpike's financial consultants recommended the bonding firms receive fees equal to 1.3 percent of the bond issue. This percentage was slightly smaller than usual (down from the standard 1.5 to 2 percent) but the size of the float still meant record profits for some firms (particularly the local companies). The fee was negotiated with each firm before the deal was cut. The firms divided management fees of $1,984,000, meant as payment for organizing the package. In return for taking on the risk of the bond issue, which in theory could go sour and not sell, the firms split an underwriting fee of $566,000. The companies also shared $1.2 million for expenses, such as travel and telephone bills. Actual commissions, or "takedowns," from the bond float totaled $6.6 million. One firm disclosed it sought 25 percent profit from the deal after salaries and overhead had been met.

By all accounts the anointed companies realized great profits. The enriched bonding firms proceeded to kick back hundreds of thousand to the campaigns of state politicians. Senator Fumo, not even up for election in '86, received $3,000 from Russell, Rea & Zappala's political action committee, and $2,000 a piece from RR&Z's Gomulka and Charles Zappala — three weeks before RR&Z won the contract. Fumo is a banker as well as a lawyer. We might say it was time to make a little deposit with Vince. These guys don't seem to care what all this looks like. The point is, when you have legalized a system such as this, who needs bribery?

By late 1986, the fourteen no-bid bondsellers had given $300,750 in political contributions to the two gubernatorial candidates. Republican William Scranton received $178,600; Democrat Robert Casey, $122,150. You begin to see that this deal was a financial bonanza to the candidates. Vast new resources became available to incumbents. The bond issue soon meant huge contracts to selected highway builders, who were also free to donate. The public had to pay higher turnpike tolls. We got expanded, busier roads. Homeowners living near the expansions got more noise. Here is a bribed political system shooting down the fast lane, without a brake.

Thornburgh aides and the turnpike commissioners defended the no-bid awarding of these contracts by saying the bond issue contained risk. General obligation bonds, backed by the state, are said to be risk-free; they are regularly awarded by bid to firms who estimate what interest rate they can pass on to bond buyers. The turnpike bonds weren't guaranteed by the state, but were dependent on turnpike tolls. Turnpike tolls in fact were increased 30 percent on January 2, 1987, to pay for the bond issue. Turnpike officials cited the supposed element of risk as *the* crucial reason why competitive bids were avoided. "I've got to be 100 percent sure the individual doing this knows what he's doing," Ursomarso told the Pittsburgh Post-Gazette in 1986. He said they had to be sure to select known firms with "muscle" to sell bonds if the issue "threatened to fall apart." (Commissioners also argued that sweetheart awards were necessary because of the great size of the bond issue, the compressed time schedule involved, and the uncertainty of interest rates for such a large sum of money. These arguments of course were straw men, as the huge bond issue could always have been broken into smaller, more easily handled pieces.)

The argument about the bonds being fraught with risk is debatable. These bond companies don't take risks; they are as nervous as sheep with their own money. Pennsylvania turnpike bonds are about as sure a public investment as you'll find. They merely jack up the tolls and let the drivers pay for the contractors' and the politicians' windfalls. (This is also why, you begin to see, they're so nervous about the possibility of bad publicity hurting revenues. A serious boycott might cause the whole shebang to fall like a house of cards, literally hurting everybody, and his brother.) Turnpike bonds *always* made money, and have never come close to even a suggestion of default. In fact, turnpike bond issues have regularly been retired or refinanced *early*. If there is anything risky about the whole business it's the bond investors themselves. Recall that the bond investors in the 1930s would not buy into the untried Pennsylvania turnpike, and the project had to be financed by Franklin Roosevelt. These guys don't take risks, and they aren't around to help when they're really needed. They only put down their money on sure payoffs. In this case they bet on both parties' politicians, who'd receive hundreds of thousands of dollars from these firms, and who'd defend their actions by putting forward the ridiculous canard about these no-bid bonds being fraught with risk. Both parties were paid off, so neither party kicked.

Several turnpike bond issues have been floated since 1986, each with more or less similar rules of engagement. In 1989 some $240 million in no-bid bonds were sold to finance various projects and refinance others. In August 1992, $570 million in bonds were sold, this time solely to refinance earlier bond issues. In all, according to The Bond Buyer's tally, RR&Z became senior manager for all four turnpike bond issues between 1988 and 1992, totaling about $1.4 billion.

The prospectus for the 1992 issue reveals the by-now familiar cast of characters. Russell, Rea & Zappala is the main underwriter. Two dozen or so other firms make the list, including Scheetz, Smith & Co. (Republican Malone's favorite); big companies such as Dean Witter, Kidder Peabody, PaineWebber, and Legg Mason; and smaller concerns such as Shelby, Kern, Frederick & Shelby, of Western Pennsylvania. Merrill, Lynch isn't listed. For bond counsel we have the obligatory two firms, one for each party; again Flaherty & Sheehy of Pittsburgh, and Buchanan, Ingersoll. This time around there's an added surprise. "Certain legal matters," reads the prospectus, "will be passed upon for the underwriters by Astor, Weiss & Newman," (senator Fumo's law firm) and "Cohen & Grigsby," which is the firm of Thornburgh pal Evans Rose.

So now it's not enough that each party has to have its own counsel, and all the inefficiencies, duplication and added expense entailed. Now each party has *two* bond counsels.

What about the kickbacks to the politicians? Records filed with the state bureau of elections make interesting reading. They indicate Russell, Rea & Zappala's in-house political action committee, the Committee for the Advancement of State and Local Government, has given more than a half million dollars to politicians. In the six and some odd years from January, 1987 to early 1993, RR&Z's PAC donated $545,805.07 to political candidates or committees. The contributions traveled all over the political and geographic map.

The Committee for Advancement of State and Local Government

contributed an average of $90,967.51 a year. The biggest single year for contributions was 1991, when $126,999 was dumped into political coffers (this was the year before the turnpike's 1992 $570 million bond issue). The second biggest year was 1989, which saw $111,275 contributed. This was the same year the turnpike floated $240 million in bonds. Off years for big bond floats, such as '87 and '88, saw contributions of only $68,906 and $57,275, respectively. RR&Z's PAC gave $77,995.30 to candidates in 1992.

Which politicians or groups were the biggest winners of these profits? A selected list includes:

Governor Bob Casey (Democrat)	$47,000
Philadelphia mayor Ed Rendell (Democrat)	$23,500
Attorney general Ernie Preate (Republican)	$19,200
State senator William Lincoln (Democrat)	$15,150
New Jersey Republican State Committee	$14,200
PA Senate Republican Campaign Committee	$12,900
PA Democratic Senate Campaign Committee	$11,675
State treasurer Catherine Baker Knoll (Democrat)	$12,000
State senator Vincent Fumo (Democrat)	$10,200
State senator Robert Jubelirer (Republican)	$ 7,200
PA Democratic State Committee	$ 4,500
PA House Democratic Campaign Committee	$ 4,400
Auditor general Barbara Hafer (Republican)	$ 3,750
PA Republican State Committee	$ 3,000
State senator Robert Mellow (Democrat)	$ 2,900
Judge Ralph Cappy	$ 2,500
Lt. governor Mark Singel (Democrat)	$ 2,300
State Rep. William DeWeese (Democrat)	$ 1,500
PA House Republican Campaign Committee	$ 600

Contributions were tendered to Philadelphia and Pittsburgh mayors Wilson Goode and Richard Caliguiri, when they were in office. A couple thousand dollars went to the Allegheny County Democratic caucus. Donations began flowing out of state, demonstrating RR&Z's growing strength and desire to compete nationwide. Many contributions went to candidates and committees in New Jersey, some to West

Virginia, and some to Alabama, including a $1,000 donation to George Wallace, Jr., in 1988.

Records show that almost all the money donated by the Committee for Advancement of State and Local Government came from either a partner of Russell, Rea & Zappala, or an employee. Some of the employees, state records indicate, made their "contributions" in the form of "payroll deductions." Part of one's salary, then, is automatically returned to the politicians, who make the salary possible. Among the employee donations was $400 donated on October 14, 1987, by an individual identified as "Gregroy (sic) R. Zappala, Investment Banker." A $305.69 contribution to the PAC on December 4, 1989, is shown as having been tendered by one "G. Zappala, Investment Banker." These contributions presumably were made by justice Stephen Zappala's son, Gregory R. Zappala, who works for RR&Z. The lines between RR&Z, the Zappalas, and the turnpike commission continue to blur, until it starts to look like one big family concern.

The above figures don't even include private contributions that may have been made by partners or employees of the investment firm. Contributions to Republican senator Jubelirer, for example. A Donald Rea is listed as giving Jubelirer $300 in 1990. The firm of (C. Andrew) Russell, (Donald E.) Rea and (Charles) Zappala, in 1991, gave Jubelirer another $300. RR&Z, you recall, is supposedly a Democratically sponsored firm. The Zappala's are political allies of Democratic senator Fumo, who at least in theory is a political adversary of Republican Jubelirer. Yet they take politically sustaining contributions from the same people. Both senators cooperate to break the law by violating the *Rutan* decision. Fumo, the democrat from Philadelphia. Jubelirer, the Republican from rural Altoona. On the surface you can't image greater contrasts. When you look into the similar actions of these two men, you begin to see two heads of the same coin. Like any two-headed coin, it's a fixed flip. Not a clean game. Maybe they're Siamese twins, joined at the hip. Certainly joined at the wallet.

I took the advice of turnpike employees and focused on the campaign contributions to senators Fumo, the Democrat, and senator Jubelirer, the Republican.

Jubelirer's disclosure included numerous contributions from Deborah Kovel, the turnpike's assistant deputy executive director for fare collection, hired in violation of *Rutan* in October 1991. Records indicate that from 1990 to 1992 Kovel gave Jubelirer $352.80, including an entry for $88.80 described in the reports as "reimbursement for hotel accommodations." Sam Carnabuci, the Republicans' patronage chief at the turnpike, donated $500 to Jubelirer in 1990. The turnpike's Bortz family donated often to the Republican senator. George, John, Natalie, and Jeff Bortz forked over a total of $1,525 from '90 to '91. Jeffrey Hess, named assistant director of turnpike purchasing in February 1992, kicked in $300 in September '91. Various members and employees of the firm Shelby, Kern, Frederick & Shelby, listed as bond underwriters in the turnpike's 1992 $570 million bond deal, gave Jubelirer a total of $1,200 in late 1991.

Fumo's returns are at least as entertaining. His law firm, Astor, Weiss & Newman — which commissioner Dodaro, I'm told, regularly designates for turnpike legal work and which was one of the four bond counselors named in the 1992 prospectus — gave $4,000 to Fumo in 1992, according to state records. Joseph Tarantino donated $600 in 1990. Tarantino is the former real estate colleague of turnpike associate executive director Mike Palermo, and the realtor who sold the turnpike its new eastern regional headquarters. Harrisburg attorney Edward Finkelstein, said to be Fumo's friend, gave $400 in March and $200 in October 1992. The turnpike in 1993 began renting office space from Finkelstein on Harrisburg's Route 22. Buchanan Ingersoll Professional Corp., the Republicans' choice for co-bond counsel in 1992, gave Democrat Fumo $1,000 in April and $500 in November 1992.

How is this game played? In the spring of 1990, when he was executive director of the turnpike, Louis Martin gave Democrat Fumo $100 and Republican Jubelirer $150.

Keep in mind that the above mentioned "donators" are only a small sampling of a small sample. The turnpike is only one piece of state government. Fumo and Jubelirer are only two of nearly 300 Pennsylvanian public servants (including our federal caucus) who play by the same rules. There are of course hundreds more in local government. Each incumbent in Harrisburg and Washington annually receives hundreds, or thousands, of individual contributions. Some contributions may seem small — those for $100 or $500, for example. But when you can dependably pull in that much from hundreds of contractors and state employees it quickly adds up. It becomes difficult, and expensive, for a challenger to beat you at the polls.

One employee at the bureau of elections made it a point to tell me that there are, as of March 1993, 636 candidate fundraising committees in Pennsylvania. More alarming, there are 1,074 political action committees registered in the state. Often one PAC will donate to another PAC, making contributions very difficult to trace. For example, Russell, Rea & Zappala's PAC in 1992 donated $1,000 to the Berks County Unity Committee and $500 for the Fund for Pennsylvania Leadership. Where does it come from, where does it go?

Many of these PACs have altruistic sounding names, such as RR&Z's Committee for the Advancement of State and Local Government. You don't see a PAC named the Committee to Bribe and Kick-Back to Those Who Line Our Pockets, though that would certainly be refreshing. One PAC whose name caught my attention was the Harrisburg-based Citizens For A Better Commonwealth. This PAC gave contributions totaling $34,850 in 1992. Recipients included Democratic governor Casey (whose campaign received a single $10,000 from this PAC on December 31, 1992), Republican AG Preate, and various legislators, particularly Fumo. Most of the contributors to the Citizens For A Better Commonwealth identify themselves as associated with the Reading law firm of Stevens & Lee. Three contributors to this PAC — John Worthington, Bruce Zimmerman and John Simler — listed themselves as managers with Syntonic Technologies, which handles the turnpike's electronic maintenance.

These politicians are all fond of repeating the lie that there is "no quid pro quo" (their favorite denial phrase) in any of these kickbacks. They'd have us believe their contributors simply are interested in the political system and in "helping out" candidates. When these guys are out of office, unable to award public money, these "contributors" won't even toss them a crumb.

After some good witch dropped a house on Dick Thornburgh in 1991 his senatorial campaign committee ended up almost $350,000 in debt. The former United States attorney general stuck Austin, Texas political consultant Karl Rove with some $250,000 in bad debts.

Following his loss at the polls, Thornburgh mailed a folksy letter, dated Thanksgiving Day, 1991, to contributors. He acknowledged his personal responsibility for his campaign debt. "Our campaign ended with a debt," the letter informed previous contributors. "I know I must shoulder most of it, but if you could help me with a final gift of $75 or $50, I'd be grateful."

Those shoulders turned out not to be too big. Thornburgh refused to take responsibility for his debts. He was asked about this letter when he came to trial for bad debts and fraud in early 1993. Thornburgh insisted he'd never intended to take personal responsibility for his campaign debts when he signed a letter saying he knew he "must shoulder most of it."

Karl Rove told me that Thornburgh's defense in court had been to testify that, tossed into the campaign by George Bush, he hadn't known the people who'd worked on his election committee. In a case study of denial, Thornburgh blamed his senatorial defeat on the unpopularity of Bush. Rove complained to me that Thornburgh and his men displayed an amazing degree of arrogance.

In the end Thornburgh's appeal for funds fell on deaf ears. In the last half of 1992, Thornburgh's committee listed contributions of only $122. That's *one hundred and twenty-two dollars.* (I personally know a man who gave ten dollars to this lost cause. For five dollars I will sell you his name.)

Thornburgh had only fair-weather friends, who'd found themselves so burdened by all the "no-quid-pro-quo" contributions they were making to current office holders that they couldn't throw poor Dick a bone. Politicians remaining in office must worry some good witch might drop a house on them.

9
Democracy's Children

Not too long ago I took my three-year-old daughter through the rotunda of the state capitol. I lifted her on my shoulders under the dome. She pointed high, and had me read aloud William Penn's hopeful words circling the heights of the rotunda: "There may be room there for such a holy experiment. For the nations want a precedent. And my God will make it a seed of a nation. That an example may be set up to the nations. That we may do the thing that is truly wise and just."

It would be nice to say I take my daughter along to the capitol for shock value, but I really bring her because I can't afford day care. It's upwards of $500 a month these days, almost a mortgage payment. One state senator we visited seemed at a loss to see a child. Not so women. A woman will almost always flash a look of understanding, and often run off for a pen and some paper to occupy the child. Women understand what it is to have to work and care for a child. Older men think it's done by magic.

That day I noticed people like to linger in the rotunda. My daughter enjoyed the ornamentation of the old capitol. Underfoot she studied the intricate brick mosaics of native bugs, birds and beasts. Wildlife aside, the rotunda's decor is a tribute to the people who founded and built democracy here. Overhead in the dome and underfoot in the bricks, colorful paintings and mosaics depict the pioneering activities of the people who built the commonwealth. Drawings of farmers working the rich land, miners digging the coal, printers working their presses, oil men greased from their derricks. It struck me that I've never seen such beings at toil in the capitol. A more truthful series of paintings might be commissioned for today's rotunda, I thought. Paintings of lawyers in alligator shoes. Friezes of affluent lobbyists with three-piece suits or Gucci bags. Dark depictions of rows of vacant buildings, with empty windows winking at the poor who sleep in the streets. A mosaic of your average Pennsylvanian before a television, an uninvolved witness to a dying experiment.

One day when I visited the rotunda a group sat at a table promoting "freedom of choice" in public education. They peddled the voucher system, in which parents would get a thousand dollars or so to send their child to the school of their choice, even to a private school. To a poor family a thousand dollar voucher is useless, as they still couldn't afford the remainder of the tuition to send their children out of the neighborhood. They would have access only to a diminished public school.

The paintings in the rotunda of our ancestors' hard work and sacrifice mock today's reality. The contributions made by eighteenth and nineteenth century Pennsylvanians — universal education, planned cities, libraries, equal access to government and justice, a reforming penal system — are today being disassembled.

If anything Pennsylvania government has grown more insulated, in deed and in symbol, from average Pennsylvanians. In time my daughter and I sauntered over to the most recent architectural addition to the capitol — a gelded, granite office annex for our representatives. Compared to the main capitol it is artistically unadorned. People don't seem to linger there, but hurry by. The public spaces of the annex seem designed to move you along. The addition to me always seems cold and uninviting. It was erected with a requisite graft scandal. We heard uninvestigated hints of political kickbacks involving its granite blocks. A young man who happened by told me, "They spent lots of money on the addition, but it's not as nice as the old part of the building."

Occasionally I'll see ordinary people hanging around the granite and the fountains outside, maybe even sticking their feet in the water, but they often seem to be looking over their shoulders as if fearing the owners will kick them out. I've heard jokes that the new marble annex is a good place for a toga party. The interior design of unadorned marble and brass trim reminds one of my friends of an expensive hotel. The legislators have commissioned for themselves a cold display of corporate architecture. It's something you'd expect to find at world headquarters of a Fortune 500 company. No matter how long you work at the company, it's never going to be *yours*. In the back of your mind you always know it. Government in Pennsylvania by the hour moves farther from the people.

One day at the capitol, walking along with my daughter, I wondered what sort of an example William Penn would say today's Pennsylvanians are setting for the rest of the country, and the world.

One evening at a social gathering a state library employee happened to tell me that some books, orphaned from a decent home at the state library, may have found their way to the incinerator. Images of midnight book-burning bonfires in 1930s Berlin danced through my turnpike-shenanigan-wearied mind. No, the concerned librarian told me, the destruction of books in the state library was much more banal. An obscure state surplus law forbids giving or selling unwanted library books to the public. The library was filled, and unwanted books — mostly decades old — were being discarded. He feared they were ending up with other refuse in the incinerator.

I dropped by the library and found a flyer containing the following information: "The State Library of Pennsylvania traces its beginnings to 1745, when Benjamin Franklin, clerk of the Colonial Assembly, was directed to order from England copies of statutes and other works for use by members of the Pennsylvania Provincial Assembly." Among its nearly one million volumes, the state library houses a remarkable collection of antiquarian and illuminated books, including some printed by Franklin. The collection is housed not far from the capitol rotunda in a grand, but antiquated, building.

I telephoned the state department of education, which administers the library. Gary Tuma, a spokesman for the department, promised to make inquiries. The library, he learned, reached its capacity sometime in the 1960s. Engineers examined the structural integrity of the building sometime in the 1980s. They ordered weight off the floors. Librarians began moving books into the basement. Many duplicate titles, said Tuma, were in the collection, and "it occurred to people that we can dispose of some of the duplicate titles to make space."

In early 1992, "when recycling was the thing," he said, the duplicates were placed in recycling bins. This practice was stopped after a month or so, he said. I asked why it was stopped. He said he wasn't completely sure, that someone had decided recycling the books wasn't a good idea. Perhaps the librarians were upset to see people rummaging for books in the recycling bins. He said something about how some of the books, in the process of being rummaged by the public, may have been thrown in nearby garbage bins....

In any event, he said, books were no longer subject to "recycling." One hundred and fifty-seven cartons of unwanted books now filled the basement of the library.

One problem, he explained, involved the obscure state surplus law. The statute forbids the state library from distributing its used books to anyone but state correctional institutions or another state agency. Library overseers were now considering asking for legislation to change the law. Perhaps, I suggested, the state library, like all other public libraries, could sell its old books inexpensively on a table in the lobby. Perhaps books could be donated to charitable groups, such as those ubiquitous and socially dangerous university women who regularly hold used book sales. Any concerned state legislator, Tuma pointed out, could propose the legislation.

The real problem is that the state library needs bigger, more up-to-date quarters, he said. "I think there's a general agreement that a new library would be good but the current economic climate seems to prohibit that," Tuma told me. "How much would a new building cost?" he asked me.

I explained I had been studying the Pennsylvania turnpike, whose new regional headquarters cost more than two million dollars. Where would one come by money like that these days? he asked.

I told him there seemed to be some experts on that subject at the turnpike.

What portrait begins to emerge of the state of democracy in Pennsylvania, the seed of our nation, the example to nations? Our politicians break the law by ignoring the U.S. Supreme Court's *Rutan* decision, and who knows what else. They award billions in no-bid contracts to their friends, and their friends kick back millions to our politicians. All at a great loss of efficiency and the cost of millions of public money. Those not lucky enough to have friends in high places are further disempowered.

Following the 1992 election the Democrats gained control of the state senate, by a margin of one seat. Republican Jubelirer found himself no longer president pro tempore. Democrat Fumo of Philadelphia rose to the chairmanship of the appropriations committee. Democrats, now in control, gloated over their new, plusher offices and approved several hundred thousand dollars in pay raises for their senate staff. The Democrats in the house, meanwhile, proposed raising their salaries to $55,000 a year, almost *three times* the $19,128 per capita income of Pennsylvanians, as estimated by the U.S. Commerce Department for 1991. In spring 1993 the leadership of the General Assembly further displayed a keen sense of the public mood by entertaining motions to recess from July to November, so members could go home, make money and campaign for another term.

Democrats now control both legislative bodies and the governor's office, but there has been little substantial legislation produced this year. Why is that? The political action committees and other contributors are throwing tons of money at the General Assembly. If these contributors can't change things more to their liking, at least they can pressure their purchased politicians to maintain the lucrative status quo.

Republicans, meanwhile, offer no real alternative. The senate Republicans' chief counsel, Stephen MacNett, loudly mourned the loss of eighteen staff jobs in the senate due to the Democratic takeover. He said nothing about the thousands of ordinary Pennsylvanians who remained without work, without health care, without homes. MacNett's wife, meanwhile, continues as one of the state legislature's biggest lobbyists. In 1993, Kathryn Speaker MacNett listed her clients as Aetna Life and Casualty; American Cancer Society; Athletic Trainers Society; Beer Wholesalers Association; Browning Ferris Industries; Buchanan Ingersoll; CEO Venture Fund; Communications Alliance; Dow Elanco; Economic Development Association; Horticultural Society of PA; Hospital Association of PA; PA Society of Hospital Pharmacists; Marine Spill Response Corp.; National Medical Care, Inc.; Medical Society of PA; Mental Health/Mental Retardation Community Centers, Inc.; Motorcycle Industry Council; National Hemophilia Assoc.;

Panhandle Eastern Corp.; Associated Pawnbrokers; Philadelphia
Eagles; Philadelphia 76ers; Philadelphia Flyers; Philadelphia Phillies;
Propane Gas Association; Rail Corporation; PA Association of
Realtors; Rodale Press; Safe Buildings Alliance; The Spectrum;
Technology Council; Travelers Express; Video Lottery Technologies
and West Publishing Company. How can some of these clients co-
exist in the same lobbying portfolio? Rodale Press, a national leader in
preventive health care, for instance, supposedly opposes alcohol con-
sumption — yet their lobbyist MacNett also carries water for the state
Beer Wholesalers Association. Other conflicts are more serious. With
so much lobbying money from heath care groups presumably flowing
into the household of the senate Republicans' chief counsel, you must
wonder if the average Pennsylvanian will get a fair shake when it
comes to health care reform. Kathryn Speaker MacNett is one of
1,149 lobbyists registered with the commonwealth in 1993. Many
enjoy close family ties to state officials, or were former legislators or
officials themselves.

Our commonwealth all the while continues to suffer. Our public
libraries, once the glory of the world, have run out of shelf space, even
as they lack the funds to buy more books. Our public schools, once
the pride of the world, decay. Democracy's children, faced with hope-
less futures, die in the streets in obscene numbers.

The public school system in Philadelphia, like the city itself, has
reached the crisis point. The state department of education ruled in
early 1993 that Philadelphia high school students weren't receiving
enough "instructional hours." In response, to meet state requirements,
Philadelphia public school administrators cut high school lunch periods in half, and declared the resulting twenty minute study halls
"instructional time." This in a system that measures educational
attainment in hours and days, like prison sentences, rather than mea-
suring one's ability to read, to add, to think. (As I write, Outcome
Based Education has become the rule for Pennsylvania. It may yet be
scuttled by formidable opponents, including many state teachers.)

In Philadelphia, in 1993, the public schools face a $22 million
deficit, Paul Hanson, a spokesman for the district, told me. In 1994
the deficit is projected to be $60 million, he said. In late April 1993,

the school administrators proposed meeting some of the budget short-fall by eliminating extracurricular activities such as music, drama, and all sports, including football, basketball, baseball and wrestling. For many of these inner-city kids sports have sadly been the only way out. Now even that shaky rung on the escape ladder is threatened.

Now that Fumo was senate appropriations chairman, I asked Hanson, what has the senator done to help the schools and children in his district? Hanson's silence told volumes. He dodged the question, saying school officials were hopeful that the city's elected representatives would yet help.

The unspoken truth is that Fumo and our other "public servants" are too busy awarding illegal patronage and no-bid bond deals, counting campaign contributions and fighting over perks. Fumo also spends time crusading to bring casino gambling to Pennsylvania. Casinos have been secretly buying dock sights in Philadelphia in hopes that riverboat gambling will be legalized. Fumo told a luncheon in May 1993 that casino gambling in Pennsylvania would already be legal if governor Casey was not "on a religious kick." Fumo was quoted as saying, "when we get a more enlightened missionary as governor we may very well see riverboat gambling." Just what we need. Gambling in Atlantic City has only brought an increase in organized crime and further degradation of the city. What an enlightened missionary would see is that more school children in Philadelphia might know how to read if Fumo would get off his gambling parlor, illegal patronage, cronyism and law firm kickback kick.

With so much tender thoughtfulness spent on behalf of Bally Casinos, senator Fumo doesn't seem to have much spare energy to help the kids in his district. Somewhere along the line he seems to have forgotten his own despair when he was a down-and-out young man, and his promise for reform.

Maybe senator Fumo could teach the kids to float bonds. Maybe school children should hire a well-connected lobbyist. Maybe the appropriations chairman can vote the kids a bag of nickels and one of those high-rollers' bus and dinner packages to Atlantic City. Maybe then they'll at least get a decent lunch.

As our schools and libraries go to hell, the state's homeless shelters remain perpetually full. One of my friends, Richard Kearns, works with local agencies attempting to shelter the homeless in Harrisburg. He tells me rising homelessness began to overload the city's shelters in 1989 and 1990. "Before then what usually happened was that the city shelters would have a slack period in the spring and summer months," he told me. "But starting in '89 and '90 that slack period didn't come. The shelters now are filled year round. What's needed isn't more shelters, but more affordable, permanent housing."

It's not that housing isn't there. Countless boarded-up homes decorate Pennsylvania cities. The 1990 U.S. census counted 24,590 houses in the capital city alone, with occupants in only 21,520 units. That's 3,070 empty houses — greater than a ten percent vacancy rate. Statewide the problem's just as bad. Out of 4,938,140 housing units in Pennsylvania, the census counted only 4,495,966 occupied homes. That's more than 442,000 empty homes across Pennsylvania. Huge vacancies exist not only in housing, but also in commercial space. In 1990 a realtors' group commissioned the planning office of Dauphin County, which includes Harrisburg, to inventory vacant commercial buildings. Randy Heilman, of the planning commission, told me vacancies were high and the realtors never published the study. They apparently feared property values would tumble if the public realized the immensity of the problem.

"White man can make anything, he just can't distribute it," Sitting Bull once observed. We have wonder medicines, but people can't get them. We have unimagined resources of knowledge, while our libraries are in trouble. We are up to our necks in empty buildings, but we won't house the homeless, or convert empty space into day care centers. We're awash in lonely elderly, many who are financially well off but who won't sacrifice a cent of their public largesse. Our children have the shortest school year in the industrial world, with three idle months in the summer, a holdover from nineteenth century farming life when kids were needed to work in the fields. Can't we provide incentives for those elderly and those students to care for our preschoolers, so that their parents can work and make a contribution?

Pennsylvania was built, as the state capitol's artwork reminds us, by forebears who harnessed abundant resources. Why is there no legislative effort to harness today's vast unused resources — both capital and human — for the common wealth?

Here in Pennsylvania, the rebirthingplace of democracy, the seed of the nation, the example to nations, we can truly count all those who fight for democracy around the world — who risk their lives for equality and justice — our children, our brothers and sisters.

What example have we set for our children, not only here, but around the world? In August 1991, while our purchasable politicians steadfastly refused to abandon selfish patronage, Boris Yeltsin climbed onto a tank in Moscow and made a stand for democracy. In so doing he became our brother, a child of our ideals. By night Muscovites held their ground against tanks, armed only with homemade gasoline bombs and their ideals. They threw off party elitism so they could decide their own lives. In so doing they became our brothers and sisters, children of ideals born here. They stood up for us.

In Italy, while Pennsylvania politicians perfected ways of ignoring the law and lining their pockets and the pockets of their friends, the mafia killed two magistrates. The two took a stand against murderers, and exerted the rule of law, and the people. One magistrate was repaid with a bomb crater big enough to hold a circus tent. He was our brother. A child of the ideals that are dying here. He stood up for us.

Around the world the people are taking a look at democracy, at the promise of equality and justice. We are being weighed, and we are being found lacking. Around the world we see sectarian violence, greed of clans, and privilege.

We in Pennsylvania, and America, could light a fire of hope. We could lead by setting an example of fairness, equality, tolerance, and sacrifice for the common good. We could speak up for the promise of universal betterment and the true spirit of justice. We could stand up for the dignity of all people.

No one in our legislature seems to know the moment. At this hour the commonwealth has denigrated into a closed, self-perpetuating system of enrichment for established clans. Why would any oppressed people in the world want to be like us?

Part 2: ≈≈

Running to the Rock for Rescue

One of these days
When you hear a voice say 'come'
Where you gonna run to?
You're gonna run to the rock for rescue
There will be no rock
                    —*The Slickers*

10

When the Levee Breaks

Lawsuits stopped illegal hiring practices at the turnpike in the 1970s, I knew, and it will probably be lawsuits that stop the current patronage violations. I spoke with a knowledgeable person about the process one might follow to file a lawsuit. "It would help if the individual was qualified for the job," my conversant said with a smile. A qualified person who lost a job to a political insider should first find an attorney. Find a big law firm, I was told, one with deep pockets. Pennsylvania's politicians had a great vested interest in patronage, dating back more than two hundred years. They're not going to give it up without a fight. They're going to drag their heels as long as they can, through as many expensive appeals as they can, my conversant suspected.

"And you should file a suit in federal court. There's no use going through the state courts."

"Why not?" I asked.

My conversant smiled.

"Because Zappala's on the supreme court. His brother's the turnpike bond dealer. Justice Zappala is the turnpike's judge." Justice Zappala, I was told, had been asked to help the turnpike in a case. What's more, justice Zappala's son handles turnpike legal work. "It's useless to fight the turnpike through the state courts."

The turnpike's lawyers in 1989 had been in a pinch and had called justice Zappala, who issued an unusual "quick order" on behalf of the commission, I'd learn. The case then was given an accelerated hearing before the high court. The order concerned a contract for a turnpike improvement underwritten by the justice's brother. Making the potential conflict worse, I was told, commissioner Dodaro, family friend of the bond underwriter and former law partner of the justice, had been involved in contacting Zappala. Having knowledge of this inside justice, my conversant was convinced that the state courts could not be relied upon for impartiality when it came to upholding *Rutan*, or other proceedings against the turnpike.

That was how, in November 1992, I started hearing complaints that the turnpike had a house judge.

Only a few weeks later, state supreme court justice **Rolf Larsen** accused his fellow jurist, justice Stephen Zappala, of fixing multiple cases to the benefit of his bond underwriter brother, Charles Zappala.

Larsen's charges were the latest installment in a cascading series of events that would be high comedy if so many people's lives weren't at stake. Pennsylvanians are learning a lot these days about the inner workings of our legal and political system. We are receiving a lesson in why the business dealings of our government officials need much tighter control, and why our justice system needs a lasting divorce from politics. We're also learning about the dangers of media concentrated into a few hands.

Pennsylvania state supreme court justice Rolf Larsen was born in Pittsburgh in 1934. After a stint in the army, he attended Penn State, the University of Pittsburgh, Duquesne University School of Philosophy, the University of Santa Clara School of Law, and Dickinson School of Law. For thirteen years he was a sole-practitioner, concentrating in personal injury and domestic relations law. Election to a ten-year term on the Allegheny County Court of Common Pleas came in 1973. In 1977 he won a seat on the state supreme court.

Controversy has marred Larsen's supreme court term. In his first term he was accused of making ethnic slurs against justice Nix. When Nix ran for re-election in 1981, The New York Times published an article saying the justice faced an unusual undercurrent in his campaign, particularly since he was unopposed on the ballot. Larsen, the Times reported, denied threatening to publicize that Nix was black. A review board cleared Larsen of the racial slur charges, and other charges that he misused his office for political ends.

Larsen has had growing difficulties with the media. The state Judicial Inquiry and Review Board, in a summation of the recent complaints, noted that, "From 1964 to 1980, justice Larsen received, periodically, highly laudatory coverage by the press; however, from 1980 to the present, coverage in major newspapers such as the Pittsburgh Post-Gazette and the Philadelphia Inquirer has been almost uniformly negative. Justice Larsen's suit for defamation and related claims against those papers remains pending.

"Despite considerable adverse publicity concerning the substance of (recent charges) and adverse publicity relating to charges dismissed by the JIRB in previous proceedings," the review board sums up, "Pennsylvanians voted to retain justice Larsen for another ten-year term in November, 1987."

Larsen's current troubles stem from two allegations of misconduct filed against him in September 1987, by Allegheny County Court of Common Pleas judge Eunice Ross. The charges were filed with the state Judicial Inquiry and Review Board, which is charged by Pennsylvania's constitution with investigating complaints and making disciplinary recommendations to the state supreme court. On October 3, 1988, three more charges against Larsen were added. These charges concerned allegations of improper conduct leveled by Allegheny County Court of Common Pleas judge Emil Narick.

Judge Ross's complaint to the judicial review board stems from a visit made by Larsen to her chambers on May 30, 1986. A Dickens' novel could be driven by all the charges of conflict-of-interest that tangle this story. At the time Ross was hearing a bankruptcy case involving the estate of the late Homer Douglas Francis. While Francis was alive his bankruptcy attorney had been Robert Lampl of Pittsburgh. After Francis's death in September 1982, his sister, Barbra Vanyo, and attorney Jon Botula, were named co-administrators of the estate. The co-administrators were slow to provide an accounting. In time it was learned that Vanyo had received a favorable real estate conveyance from the estate, while attorney Botula, a creditor to one of the late man's business interests, had taken a $200,000 loan from the assets without court approval, and had received improper preference in the repayment of a loan made to the bankrupt. Judge Ross deposed Vanyo and Ross as administrators, citing conflicts of interest. She appointed a new administratrix, who was charged with providing a fresh accounting of the estate.

In January 1986, the new administratrix and the court asked attorney Lampl to explain why he shouldn't return some $17,500 he had spent for Francis as his attorney in the bankruptcy before Francis's death. Lampl was represented at this hearing by attorney James Ashton. Ashton had recently been reinstated to the bar following disbarment for a felony conviction "brought on by alcoholism." Ashton and Lampl now shared office space, referred cases to each other, and sometimes worked as co-counsel. Larsen had befriended Ashton in 1983, during Ashton's "struggle with alcoholism and battles with cancer after his reinstatement to the bar," according to review board testimony. Ashton has had a colorful past, replete with a real skeleton in the closet. Pittsburghers still talk about the time, some years ago, when Ashton found on his property the dead body of a "mob-type character" named Abe Zeid.

On May, 30, 1986, Larsen visited Ross in her chambers for a discussion witnessed only by the two. The accounts of the visit would come to be sharply disputed by the two, with each judge coming to call the other a liar.

Larsen would say he'd paid the visit following complaints he'd heard about Ross from a third judge and others, "including particularly negative comments he had overheard in the steamroom at his club. He indicated that he communicated these matters to her as a friend and concerned colleague, and that he was not making any accusations himself."

The third judge, who was the administrator of Ross's division, testified he in fact had "discussed various concerns regarding judge Ross's judicial conduct directly with judge Ross, and that as his discussion with her had not been productive, he discussed the same concerns with justice Larsen in the hope that justice Larsen would intervene informally.... It has been common practice in Pennsylvania," notes the review board report, "and other jurisdictions, for judges to informally notify or admonish colleagues regarding complaints circulating about their personal or professional conduct."

Larsen told the review board that "none of the complaints involved good cause to believe judge Ross had committed ethical violations which would be required to be reported to disciplinary authorities;

but, the complaints and concerns, if left unaddressed, could have affected her personally, professionally, and politically." After the meeting, Larsen testified, "he recalled receiving a call from judge Ross later that day or shortly thereafter, in which she seemed quite concerned and asked if justice Larsen thought anyone would press a formal complaint against her; and that he reassured her that he thought that was unlikely."

Ross remembered a completely different meeting. After some judicial small-talk, she testified, Larsen told her, "Listen, I met two guys on the street and they said to tell judge Ross in the Homer Douglas Francis case that (attorney) Jon Botula took all the money and used it to buy a condominium in Florida." She said she told Larsen that he was incorrect about the condo, and proceeded to list for Larsen "who got what, including the $17,000 which went to attorney Lampl, but that justice Larsen replied, 'You are doing a good job, but Jon Botula is the one, you go after Jon Botula.'" Shortly after this disputed meeting, Ross testified, she did telephone Larsen, but only to ask if his anonymous sources would come forward, a request which she says Larsen declined.

In the days following this meeting Ross spoke with two attorneys about Larsen's "tip," including, on June 9, 1986, a telephone conversation with U.S. attorney for the Western District of Pennsylvania, Alan Johnson, whose notes and recollections back up Ross. Ross told Johnson, both agree, that Larsen "had passed on a tip to judge Ross that he had received from two men on the street that Jon Botula had received money in the *Estate of Francis* case, and that judge Ross was reporting it to him as a tip on a possible bankruptcy fraud." Johnson forwarded this information to his white collar division dealing with bankruptcy fraud.

Almost a year passed, to April 19, 1987, when the Greensburg Sunday Tribune and Review published an article raising questions about a land deal between Larsen and a bankrupt landfill operator, Nikolai Zdrale. Zdrale had been represented in his legal travails by both attorneys Lampl and Ashton. He sold approximately thirty-five acres of land through Ashton to justice Larsen for $5,000.

Zdrale filed for Chapter 11 bankruptcy on February 1, 1983. Among his personal assets were the thirty-five acres in rural Fairfield

Township, in western Pennsylvania's Westmoreland County. The land at various times was encumbered with business liens totaling as much as $700,000. It contained several large, man-made lakes and retaining dams, which required work. Zdrale tried selling the property for years, listing it with realtors, but received no offers. Because of the liens, which far outweighed the market value of the remote thirty-five acres, he couldn't even get a loan on the land.

Running out of money, the bank creditors pushing for liquidation, Zdrale and Ashton tried harder to sell Zdrale's landfill and other property. At a chance meeting in October 1985, in front of Larsen's Pittsburgh office, Ashton mentioned the Fairfield property to the justice. Ashton testified that he knew Larsen "was interested in rural land and the land had everything (Larsen) was looking for, even though it did have problems."

Judges have an unusual interest in land. Many other investments are severely restricted. Real estate is one of the few investments specifically authorized by the Pennsylvania Code of Judicial Conduct. "Thus," writes the review board, "real estate as an investment opportunity has unique value to judges which it would not have to others who may choose freely from a wide array of investment opportunities forbidden to judges."

Ashton favorably described Zdrale's property to the justice, "but noted the speculative nature of any purchase in light of the considerable outstanding liens."

Ashton took Larsen to see the property sometime between Thanksgiving and Christmas, 1985. In his opinion, Ashton told the justice, there was only a one in ten chance that Zdrale's bankruptcy liquidations would pay off the liens on the land. If the landfill was sold, Ashton appraised the judge, the Fairfield property might be cleared of its liens. The attorney did not specify a price, but left Larsen to make an offer.

Larsen testified he checked the selling price of three nearby plots, the highest having the value of $1,000 an acre. He multiplied the thirty-five acres by that price and came up with $35,000. To that he added an arbitrary $15,000 for the man-made lakes, and came up with a value to $50,000. Here's where the controversy thickens. Larsen testified he divided the estimated $50,000 value by Ashton's one-in-ten chance the liens would be satisfied, and came up with a purchase price of $5,000.

Independent appraisers told the review board the land and the lakes could have a total value of up to $42,000.

When he bought the land early in 1986, Larsen "took subject to over $180,000 in liens for liquidation" on the property, which "at all times" had "liens far in excess of the value of the property."

Ashton, it turned out, should never have offered the property for sale. Its business liens made the sale subject to bankruptcy court approval. Ashton would testify this had been an oversight, that he hadn't realized the property was on the bankruptcy schedule. Larsen would testify that he also assumed the property was purchasable, since Zdrale had filed for Chapter 11, or business bankruptcy, while Zdrale and his wife personally owned the land.

As this sale neared, prospects for selling the landfill improved, so much so that Ashton testified he advised Zdrale against selling the thirty-five acres for $5,000. (On February 17, 1986, an option was tendered offering Zdrale $1,174,000 for his landfill.)

Zdrale testified he decided to accept Larsen's offer on the second property. He did this, he testified, for various reasons. The man-made lakes covered almost ten acres of the property. The lakes were held in place by earthen dams. The dams were in bad shape. "Trees, shrubs, and especially weeping willows growing on and near the face of the dams severely threatened its structural integrity," notes the review board report. "The dam was already suffering leakage and heavy overflow and was in violation of Pennsylvania Department of Environmental Resources regulations. The lake and dams were liabilities rather than assets in that condition, and could cost between $20,000 and $30,000 to repair, which is more than it would cost to install such lakes originally. There would also be an extremely high maintenance cost for such lakes." (The record shows that Larsen, in fact, not well informed, calculated the lakes as an asset.) Zdrale knew it could take tens of thousands of dollars to repair the dams and to buy insurance. He also feared liability should the levee break.

There was also an ongoing problem with vandals and arsonists. Zdrale's health was poor, and he had little money. He also didn't want to go back on his word — his gentleman's agreement with Larsen in

December 1985, when his prospects were gloomier. He figured, all in all, it was a fair price, considering the value of the land and the cost of repairing the dams. Zdrale, by the way, would testify that he hadn't known Larsen was a supreme court justice until after he'd sold him the land.

Larsen and his daughter, Nina, bought the property for $5,000 on February 20, 1986. The review board describes Nina Larsen as overseeing the interior decorating of her father's condominium and maintaining a private room there for her personal use. Three months after they purchased Zdrale's thirty-five acres, Zdrale sold his landfill, and paid every penny owed his creditors. Justice Larsen and his daughter now held clear title to the thirty-five acres.

On April 19, 1987, an article in the Greensburg Sunday Tribune and Review suggested possible impropriety involving Zdrale's land sale to Larsen. It noted Zdrale's attorneys had been Ashton and Lampl.

Reading this article, judge Eunice Ross "became convinced that justice Larsen's conversation with her a year earlier had been part of a pattern of events which indicated that justice Larsen had passed the tip on to her in an effort to aid attorney Lampl, and his attorney in the *Estate of Francis* case, Ashton, in return for Ashton's role in the Zdrale land deal."

Ross would come to allege that she believed Larsen had intervened in the Francis case to steer investigations away from Lampl and onto attorney Botula, and that attorney Ashton repaid the justice by arranging the land deal.

Ross waited about six months to report her suspicions, passing up earlier opportunities. (Ross countered she in fact had reported her suspicions to the review board's chairman judge, James Rowley, during a May 26, 1986, car ride. Rowley in turn denied this, saying he would certainly have remembered charges like that. They would have struck him "like a bolt of lightning," he testified.)

In September 1987, Ross made a formal complaint to the Judicial Inquiry and Review Board. The review board made official notice that "this was her first formal report of the incident to the JIRB, and occurred more than fifteen months after the alleged misconduct, and about six months after the April 19, 1987, newspaper article."

It was also two months before Larsen stood for re-election. On October 8, 1987, one month before his retention ballot, the Pittsburgh Post-Gazette published an article detailing Ross's charges. Still, the people of Pennsylvania re-elected Larsen.

Other complaints against Larsen began to fly home. The second complaint filed with the review board involved the justice's home.

In late 1980 Larsen purchased a $385,000 condominium atop Pittsburgh's Mount Washington. Two years later the Catholic Diocese of Pittsburgh closed its Saint Mary of the Mount School, located three houses away from Larsen's condo. About two hundred students had attended classes there, and three or four nuns once lived in a convent on the grounds.

The church in 1983 agreed to sell the property to a developer, who planned to spend about $20 million to transform the building into some fifty condos. The selling price for the old school was set at $1,765,000. For plans to proceed, the developer had to seek zoning variances, which were granted in March 1984 with no significant community opposition. Larsen became the only neighbor to appeal the granting of the variances in court, filing an appeal on March 30, 1984.

The judges on the Court of Common Pleas of Allegheny County, where Larsen's suit was heard, recused themselves on the grounds that Larsen was a former member. No party requested they recuse themselves. An out-of-county judge, Richard McCormick, heard the case.

The justice would steadfastly testify he simply didn't want the project built. He discussed with his attorney the effect of the new building "on his light, air, view, traffic, and safety," as well as Larsen's fear that the new condos "would oversaturate the market for condominiums and bring about a diminution in value of his unit." Judge McCormick would recall that Larsen "indicated that he was concerned about depreciation in value of his property and obstruction of view."

In August and early September of 1984 a series of settlement meetings, arbitrated by judge McCormick, were held between Larsen's attorney and those for the diocese and the developer. The developers had offered Larsen $100,000 to drop his case. During these negotiations Larsen's attorney "took the position that should (Larsen) desire to settle, his figure would be $500,000, but (Larsen) might not consent to any settlement." Larsen's attorney would later testify that he, and not justice Larsen, had selected the $500,000 figure, which seemed fair.

Judge McCormick urged Larsen's lawyer to accept a settlement of $350,000 — a compromise between the two figures.

Larsen's attorney, Leonard Mendelson, "convinced (Larsen) to settle by explaining to him that this would be a non-jury matter before judge McCormick should it go to trial, and judge McCormick might not disregard (Larsen's) failure to heed his settlement recommendations," Mendelson told the review board. "Mr. Mendelson also told (Larsen) that in light of his re-election efforts a few years hence, (Larsen) did not need an enemy like the Catholic Church." He said he warned Larsen that judge McCormick might also "be influenced by the fact that the church was the seller of the property..., and would be hurt financially if justice Larsen's appeal was sustained."

Larsen "reluctantly" agreed to the settlement, the review board heard.

During the negotiations the developer's attorney complained to the judge about the cost of the settlement, and testified that judge McCormick "replied he viewed it as being 'legal extortion.'"

Asked about this, McCormick would testify he didn't know whether he or the developer's attorney had used the phrase "legal extortion," but if he had, the judge said he would have meant it facetiously, meaning all this was "easy money" for Larsen. McCormick would tell the review board "he did not consider the settlement amount improper in the sense that he had often worked out settlements that he thought were unfair on one side or the other. ...In this case, he believed that the builders simply wanted to settle and move ahead with the project."

A series of draft settlement agreements was drawn up. In December 1984, to fund the settlement with Larsen, the church and the developer changed their sales agreement to reflect the church's obligation to pay half the settlement to Larsen, up to $175,000. It would come out in review board testimony that the church's attorney "and all the members of the church committee felt the $350,000 price was unreasonably high, and had extensive discussions about the propriety of the church's $175,000 reduction in price because some members thought 'a question of morality was involved.'"

There was one last hitch. Larsen wanted his money immediately, when he dropped his appeal. The developers, due to financial restraints of syndicating their project, would have no money until the sale with the church was closed. Larsen further refused to accept any money after January 15, 1985, which he originally understood to be the closing date.

The date came and went. Offers and counter-offers dragged on for months, with Larsen proposing monthly late penalties of between $10,000 to $25,000, on top of the settlement. The developer's attorney at one point met with Larsen. He told the justice the developer couldn't financially meet his demand. With more than a hint of exasperation, he told Larsen that the new condos "would enhance the value of (Larsen's) unit rather than harm it." The attorney told the review board that Larsen "answered that the issue was not diminution in value of his apartment, but what the developer could afford to pay." The developer's lawyer "replied to the effect that (Larsen) should not 'kill the goose that lays the golden egg.'"

Complications further clouded the project in May 1985 when a neighborhood couple, Mr. and Mrs. William Parry, living between Larsen and the proposed condos, petitioned to get involved in the appeal. The Parrys had moved to their new home after the zoning variances had been approved, and "they had not thought their intervention would be necessary to preserve their interests until they learned that justice Larsen was considering settlement of his appeal." Now neighbors were beginning to come out of the woodwork.

The besieged developers made no offer to the Parrys "despite the fact that (the developer) conceded that (the Parrys') property was more immediately and substantially affected by the proposed project than was justice Larsen's property for which they were negotiating compensation for damages." The developers instead chose to fight the Parrys' petition on grounds of the delay.

Larsen at first opposed the Parrys' petition as well, his attorney testified, "based upon the effect the Parrys' intervention would have on the virtually completed settlement negotiations." As a final settlement failed to materialize, Larsen threatened to drop his objection to the Parrys' intervention "on tactical grounds," the review board was told by various attorneys. "Mr. Parry was chairman of the Alcoa Corporation and his presence in the appeal might substantially lessen any adverse political consequence, as well as divide the cost of appeal." A final settlement not forthcoming, Larsen's attorney "wrote to judge McCormick and formally withdrew justice Larsen's opposition to the Parrys' intervention motion."

Judge McCormick nevertheless disallowed the Parrys' intervention in late September 1985. The Parrys appealed to commonwealth court, which further delayed settlement between Larsen and the developers.

The project was falling apart. The developer's attorney, his fees not paid, dropped out of the case.

Larsen's attorney, Mendelson, meanwhile, also withdrew. Larsen "himself took an active role in the case."

In late 1985, Mendelson had a chance meeting with late Pittsburgh mayor Richard Caliguiri, "during which the mayor told Mendelson that the church had asked him to see if he could help remove the stumbling blocks justice Larsen and Mendelson had presented to the project. Mendelson passed this message on to justice Larsen. Justice Larsen indicated he had also spoken with the mayor and that he would try to get things moving again."

While the Parry appeal was still pending, in June 1986, Larsen met with the church's attorney to ask for an extension of the February 1987, closing date between the developer and the church. An extension would be necessary due to the Parrys' action. The church's attorney told Larsen there were other possible buyers. "Justice Larsen responded that they would face similar zoning problems, likely delays, and that it would not make sense to go back to square one." The church's lawyer didn't view Larsen as trying to be helpful by requesting the extension to the developer's option, but testified he thought that Larsen "was simply trying to get his $350,000."

Still, the church granted the extension. In August 1986, Larsen now joined the position of the developer and the church and renewed his opposition to the Parrys' intervention. By the fall of 1986 commonwealth court upheld judge McCormick's denial of the Parry involvement. The Parrys didn't appeal. Now they were out of the case, leaving only Larsen, the church and the developer.

Larsen then accepted terms first proposed by the developer in April 1985. The justice agreed to accept $350,000 plus $5,000 for each month elapsed since February 1985 and the expected February 1987 closing date. This would amount to about $120,000 on top of the $350,000. Larsen characterized this as a "high ball" figure meant as a starting point for negotiations.

The new attorney for the developer seemed even less willing to dicker. He rejected Larsen's offer outright, suggesting Larsen accept only the $350,000. The negotiations stalled. In May 1987, the developer's option lapsed and was not renewed. There was a small, but noteworthy, side gambit. Mayor Caliguiri asked Larsen to acquire the plans for the condo project. Following the mayor's instructions, Larsen got the plans from the developer and passed them on to a "close friend" of the mayor's, developer Rocco Scigliano. Scigliano reviewed the plans and told the mayor the project was unsalvageable.

The developer's attorney would testify that he hadn't known the plans were passed on to another developer, that Larsen had told them they were for a potential buyer. This had left the attorney with the impression that Larsen's conduct "was calculated, nonetheless, to salvage the project and thereby aid (the developer), the church, mayor Caliguiri, and to preserve his own $350,000 settlement as well." Asked about this by the review board, Larsen "characterized this conduct as an accommodation to his good friend mayor Caliguiri, and a genuine effort to help the church."

The project was dead, and the church wasn't helped much. As of August 1989, the church property was still for sale, and the developer owed the diocese about $20,000.

Several real estate appraisers told the review board that Larsen's original assessment of $500,000 in damages was justified. Mendelson, Larsen's attorney, testified that Larsen's damage estimate was not based solely on the present value of the justice's condo, but also its future value. "(T)hus, for example, if the property in the future would be worth let's say $1 million but, as a result of this development, would only be worth $400,000, the damages would be $600,000,"

Mendelson testified.

Nevertheless, Mendelson, "admitted on cross examination that in all his extensive real estate experience he cannot recall being involved in a case where damages were almost equal to the purchase price of the property."

Larsen in this instance was accused before the review board of using the legal system as "a weapon in an attempt to coerce an inordinately large financial settlement."

One begins to see Larsen's undoing. Larsen, to judge by his physical appearance, seems slight of build, almost elfin. Make no mistake, here we have a legal bruiser who obviously knows the court system very well. Black belts in karate must register their hands as lethal weapons, golfer play with handicaps, but judges can take their personal business to court with no hands tied behind their backs.

In this case Larsen almost seems to be toying with the developers and the church. We're told of Larsen's use of "tactics," but his calculations seem cold as hard steel, with no apparent underlying sense of morality or politics. Every move is pure procedural gambit, underpinned with no apparent moral reasoning. Thus he first disapproves of his neighbors entering the case, then he backs them, then withdraws his support. He has to be warned by his attorney of the public relations danger of sticking it to the church. The problem with the church seems to weigh in his calculations only in some cold, intellectual sense. Does he *feel* what's wrong?

We're never sure if Larsen genuinely wants to kill the project. The suspicion nags us that, all along, his legal mind is pondering ways to cash in big. We begin to see a disconnection with public sentiment. Any public leader, or politician, worth his salt would know he was licked the minute the church was involved. When Father Flanagan comes around with a hat in his hands you don't use the legal system to lift out $350,000 for yourself. This doesn't look good in the movie.

Just because you can do something, though it's legal, doesn't mean you *should* do it. The more "power" you have, the less you can use for yourself. The greater you are, the more you must consider the least among us.

Larsen seems to have lost connection with the public. Not only in this dealing with the church, but in his land deal with Nikolai Zdrale. Though he had complicated legal reasoning behind his offer to purchase thirty-five acres of land for $5,000, Larsen never seems to ask himself how this is going to look. The public, in common experience, seldom sees land sell that cheap. So it was in the second complaint. When a new developer comes in, the average Joe usually gets the shaft, not $350,000.

Larsen and most public officials I've studied for this book seem to have lost their moorings. We've created a pampered, professional, permanent government class, with little in common with the average struggling American.

Each of these insensitive little things that Larsen engineered was legal. Like the raindrops piling up behind Nikolai Zdrale's levee, each alone appears to be inconsequential. But those raindrops build up, held back by a thin veneer of public trust and confidence. We're suddenly straining against the deluge that will surely come, when the levee breaks.

11

Washed Away

Justice Rolf Larsen sought help to fight the charges leveled against him. In the summer of 1985 he went to see judge Emil Narick, a senior judge on the commonwealth court. Larsen told Narick of judge Ross's charges, and asked Narick to appear as a witness for him. Larsen and Narick, several years earlier in an unrelated case, had discussed negative rumors concerning another judge, and Larsen had "interceded" with this third judge. Now Larsen wanted Narick to corroborate that the justice's visit to judge Ross, supposedly to appraise her of negative rumors, was consistent with Larsen's pattern or practice in such affairs.

Ross's charges by this time were splashing across the Pittsburgh Post-Gazette and other western Pennsylvania media. The accusation that Larsen had intervened on behalf of attorneys Ashton and Lampl, and had been rewarded with a cheap land deal from Nikolai Zdrale, was becoming household talk. Judge Narick thought back to certain encounters he'd had with the justice. Rather than testify on behalf of Larsen, he brought his recollections to the attention of the review board, with the result that three more charges were issued against Larsen.

Narick testified that, sometime in 1985, Larsen asked to meet with him and said, "You have a case before you, there's a fellow named Jay (sic) Ashton, who's an attorney reinstated to the bar and, help him out, if you can."

Narick agreed the request wasn't improper, as judges sometimes are called upon to lawfully help attorneys with courtroom skills. The only reason he had to suspect Larsen's request wasn't proper, Narick would testify, was that the justice asked to meet him outside chambers.

Sometime between March and August 1986, Larsen again asked to meet with him out of chambers, Narick told the review board. This time, he said, Larsen came to him with an odd piece of information. He testified Larsen told him Pittsburgh mayor Caliguiri had an interest in a zoning case before Narick. "I hear you," Narick testified he responded. The whole conversation lasted thirty-five to forty-five seconds, he estimated.

It was a strange request, Narick would say later, as he was a close friend to the mayor, while he shared only a cordial acquaintance with Larsen. Making matters stranger, Narick testified, Larsen hadn't indicated "on which side of the case mayor Caliguiri was interested, nor did that recalled statement indicate how favoritism was to be granted."

Once again, in June or July of 1984, Larsen arranged to meet Narick outside chambers, this time at the Rivers Club, where they both were members, Narick testified. He said that Larsen met him in the foyer of the club's locker room and presented him with a list, saying, "see what you can do about them as far as assigning to certain judges or not to certain judges." The typewritten list was one or two pages long. On the list were the names of eight to ten tax appeal cases that, Narick said, were being handled by attorney Mendelson. Mendelson at the time was representing Larsen in his condo dispute. Again Narick expressed bewilderment, as he considered himself a closer friend to Mendelson than to Larsen.

Narick couldn't remember whether Larsen had mentioned Mendelson's name in this instance, or whether he'd asked a clerk to check for the attorney of the cases on Larsen's list. He testified he hadn't preserved the list, nor had he acted on Larsen's request.

Larsen denied each of Narick's charges, and again we have the spectacle of two judges calling each other liars. Each of these complaints originating with Narick would eventually be dismissed by the review board as being contradictory and without corroboration. Had any of these events happened, the review board chastised Narick, he had violated his ethical obligation by waiting several years and not reporting them immediately. The review board seemed befuddled by its own airless reasoning. They found, on the one hand, Narick "has an excellent reputation for honesty and integrity" with no apparent motive to lie. On the other, "judge Narick's failure to report the matter promptly to this board is inconsistent with his current recollection, and his reputation as an ethical jurist." Does not compute. The review board seems unable to understand why a lower court judge might hesitate before filing a complaint against a supreme court justice.

The point is, now there was a scent of blood in the water, and sharp teeth were coming out for Larsen. Justice Larsen, expert in the law, fought the judicial inquiry and review board and its witnesses at every procedural turn. He fought with all the spirit of a man afloat on the ocean, bashing circling sharks with a plank. At one point proceedings were held up for about a year, from about April '90 to May '91, "stayed pending disposition of a special petition for an order seeking a permanent injunction barring this board from proceeding based upon alleged procedural irregularities and recusal grounds," the board reports. (Try reciting that charm next time the cops are breaking down your door, or your head.)

The preliminary investigation had begun in May 1988, evidence was heard through June 1989, and the final report wouldn't be issued until July 1991. Swift justice for everyone but judges.

Most of the charges, including the allegation that Larsen had intervened in the *Estate of Francis* case in return for a beneficial land deal, would be dismissed, mostly due to lack of corroboration or other evidence. The review board found nothing wrong with Larsen's having taken the church and the developer to court for supposed damages to his condo. Like anyone else, a judge has a right to legally pursue his private interests in court. What is legally correct may not be *politically* correct. We begin to see some of the inherent problems with a political judiciary, administered by politicians who must run for office.

In the end, the board ruled that the only provable impropriety concerned judge Ross's charge that Larsen had given her an inappropriate "tip" in the Francis estate case. The testimony of two lawyers, including the U.S. attorney, confirmed that Ross had talked to them about the incident shortly after it was alleged to have happened. The U.S. attorney, Alan Johnson, had contemporaneously referred the "tip" to his white collar division.

"We find sufficient clear and convincing evidence," reported the board, "that justice Larsen stated something to the effect that, two men on the street had told him that in the *Estate of Francis* case, Jon Botula took all the money and used it to buy a condominium in Florida."

In its deliberations the review board measured Larsen's conduct against several canons of the Code of Judicial Conduct. Canon 1 provides:

A judge should uphold the integrity and independence of the judiciary

An independent and honorable judiciary is indispensable to justice in our society. A judge should participate in establishing, maintaining, and enforcing, and should himself observe, high standards of conduct so that the integrity and independence of the judiciary may be preserved. The provisions of this Code should be construed and applied to further that objective.

Canon 2 reads:

A judge should avoid impropriety and the appearance of impropriety in all his activities

A. A judge should respect and comply with the law and should conduct himself at all times in a manner that promotes public confidence in the integrity and impartiality of the judiciary.

B. A judge should not allow his family, social, or other relationships to influence his judicial conduct or judgment. He should not lend the prestige of his office to advance the private interests of others; nor should he convey or, knowingly permit others to convey the impression that they are in a special position to influence him. He should not testify voluntarily as a character witness.

Canon 3, in part:

A judge should perform the duties of his office impartially and diligently

A. Adjudicative Responsibilities...

(4) A judge should accord to every person who is legally interested in a

*proceeding, or his lawyer, full right to be heard according to law, and
except as authorized by law, must not consider ex parte (meaning one-
sided — Editor) communications concerning a pending proceeding.*

The board ruled that Larsen had violated Canon 2. *"Ex parte* communications with a judge regarding a case over which that judge is
presiding may give rise to an appearance of impropriety which may
undermine public confidence in the judiciary," the inquiry found.
"...The reason for the prohibition of such *ex parte* communications is
illustrated here. Because the tip was presented in terms of having been
provided by an anonymous or confidential source, and because it was
communicated *ex parte,* rather than through proper channels, the tip
raised an appearance of impropriety regarding the need and/or motive
for communicating the tip *ex parte,* notwithstanding justice Larsen's
excellent reputation as a truthful, ethical, and respected jurist."

In other words, because it looked sneaky, with the potential to create the impression of partiality and unfairness, it hurt the judiciary.
"(D)espite the absence of improper motive," the board concluded,
"...the conduct by itself raised an appearance of impropriety, which
could undermine public confidence in our judiciary." This confidence
is particularly important in the supreme court, the board noted, where
appeals are final.

In the board's opinion, the justice's behavior, and court precedent,
ruled out stern treatment, such as removal from office. "We reject
entirely any suggestion of removal with perpetual disqualification or
suspension with forfeiture of office. Those sanctions are reserved for
criminal misconduct, serious and unmitigated misconduct, a pattern
of non-criminal misconduct, or repetition of misconduct previously
disciplined with lesser sanctions. Such sanctions are too plainly disproportionate to the single instance of mitigated misconduct found here
to even warrant serious discussion." Yet, "a finding of misconduct
without further penalty would seem to be disproportionate in the
opposite extreme." The board reviewed past cases, finding that "private admonishment, public censure, or brief suspensions have generally been imposed upon judges for such misconduct, with public censure being the more common sanction. A set term of suspension has
generally been reserved for a variety of misconduct of intermediate

severity. In several cases, justices of the highest courts in their respective jurisdictions have been censured or reprimanded for violations as serious as, or more serious than, the violations proved here."

The board concluded, "In light of the presence of a significant mitigating circumstance (i.e. justice Larsen's excellent character for truthfulness, integrity, and competence as a jurist), we conclude that a public reprimand is appropriate under the facts and circumstances of this case."

The review board recommended Larsen receive a public reprimand from his fellows on the state supreme court. This would be construed by some as lenient punishment.

The seven-member state supreme court found itself all-but hamstrung. Larsen of course had to recuse himself from deliberations on his own punishment. One justice, James McDermott, had died in June 1992, and was replaced by Frank Montemuro, who had sat on the JIRB during the Larsen investigation, and so had to recuse himself. Larsen had accused justice John Flaherty and chief justice Nix of bias against him, so those two disqualified themselves. That left justices Zappala, Ralph Cappy and Nicholas Papadakos.

The court was not required to follow the review board's recommendations, but did. On October 13, 1992, Zappala and Cappy voted to adopt the board's findings and reprimand Larsen. Papadakos dissented, saying the proceedings against Larsen had been tainted by procedural errors and that the case should be returned to the review board for more hearings. So it was a 2-to-1 vote.

The popular wisdom was that Larsen should have left well enough alone. But Larsen was ever litigious, never politic. On November 25, 1992, he filed a motion for reargument of his case. He didn't stop there. He went ballistic, filing a second motion requesting Zappala and Cappy disqualify and recuse themselves from proceedings. Of course, should Zappala and Cappy recuse themselves, that would leave only favorable Papadakos to vote. This unlikely and amazing single-judge scenario was largely overlooked, owing to the sensation aroused by Larsen's charges against his two fellow jurists. Larsen accused Zappala and Cappy of "at all times" acting "in concert and together" in the worst sort of political chicanery, behaving in a manner more befitting a Pittsburgh mayor than a supreme court justice.

It would be easy enough to say that his basic complaint was that his two antagonists had voted to reprimand him to hurt his chances for re-election in 1997. Or that the two wanted to prevent Larsen from one day becoming chief justice. Should chief justice Nix, born in 1928, die or retire, Larsen, by seniority, would become chief justice. Even this was swept to the background.

In a deeper sense, like so many Pennsylvanians involved in our legal system over the past few years, Larsen, between the lines, complained of unfairness. Others around him were getting away with activities that were just as bad, or worse, he seems to complain.

"Justice Zappala and justice Cappy are very ambitious," Larsen wrote in his enlightening motion, "with enormous cravings and appetites for power, and at all times each is looking to promote and enhance his political career (and each other's career where possible) by either election or appointment. Their respective cravings and appetites for power are fueled by a 'need to control.' In the world of justice Zappala and justice Cappy crave and 'need' is power for power's sake...for self-aggrandizement as opposed to power for altruistic motives. The more power they can seize, the more control they will have and the more purely 'personal' satisfaction they will enjoy."

He charged that the two continually spread their names around for "high" office to "create an illusion" that they are "political powerhouses." Zappala, he wrote, entertained notions of running for governor.

Here he mentions the Zappalas' patronage pal at the turnpike, commissioner Dodaro. "Additionally, to build their power and control," he wrote, "justice Zappala and justice Cappy have supported numerous candidates for public office including, but not limited to, James Dodaro, esquire, for attorney general of Pennsylvania.... If present Allegheny County commissioner Pete Flaherty 'goes to Washington' as is sometimes rumored, justice Zappala and justice Cappy have already stated their support for James Dodaro, esquire, to replace Pete Flaherty as Allegheny County commissioner."

Larsen added that Cappy, when he took over administration of the Philadelphia court system two years previously, appointed "good soldiers" as judges who would do Cappy and Zappala's bidding. He alleged that Cappy conspired with a go-between to help with the appeal of a criminal defendant from Pittsburgh.

He went on to paint Zappala as a conniving politician. He charged that Zappala had approached him in January 1992, and "told him that he, justice Zappala, had been in contact with the Pennsylvania legislative leaders and that they (the legislative leaders) were unhappy with chief justice Nix serving as chief justice of the Pennsylvania Supreme Court." Legislative leaders were also unhappy with the prospect of Larsen as chief justice, he said Zappala intimated. This unhappiness with Larsen and Nix, he said Zappala told him, was "impacting adversely on the court's budget and pay increases for the judiciary." Zappala, Larsen wrote, suggested a solution to this "chief justice problem" by having the legislature initiate a "constitutional amendment making the position of chief justice an elected position as opposed to a seniority position as is presently the case." This, Larsen wrote, would clear the way for Zappala to become chief justice, succeeded by Cappy, some eleven years Zappala's junior.

"This overwhelming desire for the office of chief justice on the part of justice Zappala and justice Cappy was starkly evident at the sad occasion of the funeral of justice McDermott in June of 1992," wrote Larsen. He accused Cappy of coming up to him at the funeral and referring to Nix, who was "recovering from an illness and not feeling well." Should Nix happen to die or resign, he wrote Cappy asked him, would Larsen waive his right to succeed Nix so that Zappala could become chief justice? Larsen, "knowing that justice Flaherty has more seniority than justice Zappala, responded by asking justice Cappy: 'What are you going to do with justice Flaherty, who would be next in line to become chief justice?' He says Justice Cappy responded, 'Don't worry, *we* (meaning justice Cappy and justice Zappala) will take care of him." This "lust for power, control, and the office of chief justice," argued Larsen, brought into question Zappala and Cappy's impartiality as required by judicial canon.

Larsen went on to charge that Zappala illegally tape records telephone conversations. He passed along rumors that both Zappala and Cappy wear "bodywires" to surreptitiously record personal conversations. (I should add, for the curious, that he didn't say what *was* under the justices' robes.)

As entertaining and perhaps enlightening as all this was, it was just back-room-court gossip compared to the heavy-duty charges Larsen dropped next. He accused Zappala of fixing cases. He wrote that Zappala should disqualify himself because Zappala was being investigated by the review board and "by the federal government and federal law enforcement officials, to-wit:

"Justice Zappala is alleged to have arranged for one of his brothers to receive bonding work from various local governments in the Commonwealth of Pennsylvania and through multiple 'layered corporations' justice Zappala is alleged to have received indirect 'kickbacks.'"

Larsen alleged that "Zappala's clandestine interest in the 'layered corporations' has led to his gross misconduct in certain cases before this court involving three local governments which had purchased bonding services from justice Zappala's brother — the city of Philadelphia, the county of Allegheny and the city of Pittsburgh — and where the temporary financial health of these municipalities was at risk."

Zappala, Larsen alleged, at various times had met *ex parte* with representatives of these government bodies, and advised them the "'route' and procedures to use in prosecuting" their cases in "this court." When these suits were filed "in the manner in which justice Zappala had counseled and directed, justice Zappala then took charge and 'guided' (these suits) through the Pennsylvania Supreme Court in a 'special' manner." These various cases, involving labor difficulties with the cities of Philadelphia and Pittsburgh, and Allegheny County, were subsequently resolved in favor of the governmental bodies, Larsen wrote, and against labor, "with the result that (the governmental bodies') financial strength was maintained and thus the bonds that had been handled through justice Zappala's brother, to the indirect benefit of justice Zappala, were rescued from risk and maintained their strength." As we'll see, these charges begin to ring true with observers of the turnpike.

Larsen wrote that he had dissented in these cases, exposing "flaws in the majority's reasoning," despite lobbying from Zappala for a united court. "A unanimous opinion is always less suspect than a divided or split court," Larsen illuminated. As a result of his dissent, Larsen complained, Zappala "harbors great ill will and retaliatory feelings."

One thing's certain: he was right about the ill will. Larsen's accusatory motion for Zappala and Cappy's recusal went over as well as a zeppelin filled with concrete. Pennsylvanians were soon treated to the spectacle of various justices of their supreme court calling each other crooks, liars, strong-arm terrorists and/or crazy.

On December 6, 1992, justice Cappy wrote to chief justice Nix that Larsen had "made assertions against me in his Petition for Disqualification and Recusal which not only challenge my personal integrity, but also the integrity of the Supreme Court of Pennsylvania." He noted that the code of judicial conduct prohibited him "from making public comment on any matter which is presently in litigation before me." He asked Nix to "appoint an independent ad hoc panel comprised of persons whose integrity is unquestionable" to investigate Larsen's charges and report back to the public within sixty days. "As for me," Cappy wrote, "I welcome enthusiastically the investiture of such a panel, less so for the inevitable complete demudding of my name than for the just response it will give to Pennsylvania citizens' proper demand for accountability, fair play and truth-telling."

Nine days later, on December 15, Larsen shot back by filing a supplemental petition for disqualification, in which he accused Cappy of violating Larsen's right to due process by calling for the closed, ad hoc panel rather than an open hearing. He pointed out that Cappy's self-described interest in "demudding" his own name displayed his bias against Larsen, "and thus, it is impossible for justice Cappy to be an impartial and unbiased jurist in this matter to which (I am) entitled and which is required by the U.S. constitution and the Pennsylvania constitution."

He complained that Cappy's letter amounted "to a pre-judged adjudication" of his case. He wrote that Zappala, on December 7, had "stated he was not joining justice Cappy's aforementioned letter" which called for the ad hoc panel. "Zappala specifically stated that he would handle (Larsen's petition for disqualification) in his, justice Zappala's, own way — and that he, justice Zappala had a 'long memory.'

"Later that evening," Larsen continued in his brief, "on Monday, December 7, 1992, (I) had alighted from an automobile which was stopped to the side of a private, covered driveway to a Philadelphia hotel. As (I) started to cross the said entrance driveway, a person standing in the near vicinity yelled with alarm to (me) to 'watch out.' Just (then) a vehicle commandeered by justice Zappala and operated at an excessively high rate of speed drove perilously close to (my) person in an apparent attempt to run down and physically injure (me). Except for the warning to 'watch out' (I) would have been violently struck by the speeding automobile commandeered by justice Zappala. This behavior of justice Zappala makes it beyond dispute that (he) harbors malice, ill will, bias and prejudice toward (me)."

Larsen went on to complain that, the next day, Zappala had read aloud and circulated a draft letter in which he described Larsen's petitions as having caused a "'tumultuous situation'" on the court. Zappala wrote "he would be refraining from making any public comment until the said 'Larsen matter' was disposed of; and further he, justice Zappala, stated that he had been 'advised' that this 'Larsen matter' would be resolved in six to eight weeks," Larsen reported. He complained again that he has been prejudged. Larsen asked, "Who has 'advised' justice Zappala of this predetermined, arbitrary time frame?"

The growing personal rancor between the justices is evident. Larsen's accusations about the car "commandeered" by Zappala unfortunately but predictably received by far the most media attention, almost to the exclusion of other matters. It turned out that state senator Fumo, no less, was driving the car "commandeered" by Zappala, but no witnesses came forward to support Larsen's contention that our justice risked being run over. The importance of this story, in my mind, is that it amply illustrates the low ebb between the two men. One justice had best cross the street and run in the opposite direction when he sees the other coming. The next time they would sit together in court, presiding over a hearing, Zappala wouldn't even look at Larsen.

All this proved irresistible to state attorney general Ernie Preate, who by mid-December 1992 for some reason felt compelled to appoint a special prosecutor to look into Larsen's charges. It's a measure of how low public trust has sunk in Pennsylvania that Preate was generally seen to have been running for governor by naming the prosecutor. Since few in the high ranks of the state attorney general's office have done honest public work for so long, no one can imagine that Preate was simply doing his job. Truth is, Pennsylvanians in and out of government have complained of stupefying corruption for years, but those complaints have fallen on officially deaf ears. It took a supreme court justice to yell attempted murder before people started waking up.

Preate asked the legislature for $770,000 for his special prosecutor. This request found the AG in hearings with senator Fumo, speak of the devil, now head of senate appropriations. Fumo rightly wondered why Preate needed $770,000 for this investigation, considering the AG's already bloated $60 million budget. Fumo went so far as to question the attorney general's authority to investigate the state supreme court. House speaker DeWeese chimed in that $770,000 was ridiculous. "This is not the Manhattan Project," he said. "We're not inventing the atomic bomb."

Maybe they were. At least, maybe they feared they were. DeWeese proceeded to make rumblings that he and other Democratic leaders would swiftly begin investigating the possibility of impeaching Larsen. Reporters asked if he was doing this to protect justice Zappala, a charge which DeWeese said he "categorically" rejected. Luckily for DeWeese, the reporters didn't ask the half million dollar question — or, more accurately, the $545,805.07 question (the amount of cash donated by Russell, Rea & Zappala's PAC to state politicians since 1987): "Are you doing this to protect yourselves?"

DeWeese had drawn $1,500 from the wondrous Zappala money pump. Fumo had wet his lips to the tune of $10,200. Ernie Preate, who presumed to wear the mantle of public trust so that he could look into this mess, had drunk in, over the years, $19,200, some of it in rather large chunks. Preate in fact finds himself in a dilemma. If he unearths no wrongdoing people can rightly wonder if he, for reasons of self interest, failed to plumb the deepest depths of this mud hole. If some activity should turn up which, shall we say, approaches the line of some jury's limit of propriety, people will rightly wonder whether Preate had averted his gaze all those years while he was standing in line at RR&Z pay window, with nary a squeak of complaint until now. He'll have to say he's shocked, shocked to find there's bonding going on around here. The important point that should be made is that none of these characters seems at all interested in focusing the public's attention on the true depths of this crisis. (In fact, their actions — not wanting to fund an investigation, calling for Larsen's impeachment — suggest cover-up.) The intolerable crisis of no-bid contracting and reciprocal large donations to our "public servants" is nonetheless becoming sorely evident.

In their little gambits to deep-six Larsen's charges, DeWeese and (particularly) Fumo came off looking self-serving, even scared. In the state Democratic party it's Fumo's smug and no-apologies brand of governing — blatant cronyism, boundless patronage, countless campaign contributions from state contractors — that started everybody, including and especially himself and his friend Steve Zappala, down the primrose path into this quicksand. Republican senator Jubelirer, in fairness to Fumo, is just as bad, observers tell me.

Larsen at first refused to cooperate with Preate's special prosecutor. Then came the orchestrated calls in the legislature to impeach him, though this was precisely the punishment the review board said would be the most unfair. Suddenly the legislative judicial committees awakened from their decade-long comas to consider impeaching Larsen, who'd had the temerity to suggest Fumo's pals were crooks. Legislative leaders from both parties were quick to say the judicial committees would only investigate Larsen. The committees would not look into allegations leveled against the whole court, and certainly not the legislature or its patrons. This sheds light on how the judicial committees are used as tools of bi-partisan cover-up and injustice, not honest bodies meant to uncover the whole truth of a rotten system. Much blame for the public's distrust of our legal system can rightfully be laid on the judicial committees on the state and federal levels. The members of these committees have shamefully kept their heads in the sand through one of the most corrupt periods in American and Pennsylvania history.

Seeing the growing threat of impeachment, Larsen agreed to testify before a grand jury. Attorney general Preate, for his part, told reporters he wanted to wrap up his investigation "very, very quickly." That's a safe bet.

Elevating this whole sad comedy to near divine heights, legislators in the Pennsylvania General Assembly soon raised their voices for "judicial reform." Look who's calling the kettle black here. Everyone in the legislature has been purchased by legalized kickbacks from no-bid state contractors, 1,074 political action committees, and 1,149 lobbyists. The skeptical observer must wonder which of these PACs paid the legislators to call for "judicial reform." The answer, of course, is all of them. Those who presume to own our legislature would very much like to shift the focus of all this to Larsen personally, away from the Zappalas and their cronies, and particularly away from the corrupt legislature and its wide-open practices. When you get to the bottom of it, supreme court justice Rolf Larsen and his loud mouth are just no good for the smooth conduct of business as usual.

This blow up at the state supreme court soon made Pennsylvania a national laughingstock in legal circles. Stephen Gillers, an ethics specialist and professor at New York University Law School, told the Pennsylvania Law Journal, "Perhaps this unprecedented episode gives the people of Pennsylvania an opportunity to reconsider whether they want to select members of the judiciary in another way — perhaps by appointment, rather than election, as in New Jersey." You know you're down when New Jersey looks like up.

Lynn Marks, of Pennsylvanians for Modern Courts, posed what certainly is a central question: "How would you feel if you were a litigant before them right now?" he asked the Law Journal. "Personally, I can't imagine it and that really worries me."

Other people don't have to imagine it, because they're living it. I've been writing books about the justice system since 1987, and I've spoken with many litigants, and the answer is, now more than ever, people aren't happy. It's deeper than that. The public is not only displeased with the judiciary, they're unhappy with the generations-old, festering praetorian corruption officially tolerated throughout the state. They don't like selective law enforcement, administered from what's seen as a politicized attorney general's office. They're also distrustful — no, fed up – with the revolving door between the legal profession and elective office.

In January 1993, I met with Nikolai Zdrale, the bankrupt landfill operator who'd sold Larsen the thirty-five acres for $5,000. Quiet and timid, Zdrale is a graying and gaunt man who speaks much of God and the Bible. If you think his story is already too complicated, too bad. After the sale to Larsen, Zdrale was charged with unsuccessfully planning the murder of a state department of environmental resources official, and was sent to prison. He was released, pending appeal, and says the attempted murder charges against him were trumped up in order to get him to testify against a second landfill operator. He says U.S. attorney general Dick Thornburgh's former law firm represented yet a third landfill operator. The murder charges against him were cooked up by Thornburgh's cronies, he says he suspects, in order to eliminate competition in the landfill business. He hired a private investigator. The private investigator learned that, while Zdrale was in prison, prosecutors had placed a body tap on a fellow prisoner in an unsuccessful attempt to have inmate Zdrale confess to planning the murder. The prosecution was headed by senior deputy state attorney general Lawrence Claus. Zdrale's supposed co-conspirators in the attempted murder, meanwhile, seem unreliable and keep changing their story. His conviction was overturned in early 1993, and he's now awaiting a new trial.

I met with Zdrale in a Clairton, Pennsylvania, warehouse owned by businessman John Gagliardi. Zdrale and Gagliardi filled my ears with suspicions of crooked justice. For fifteen years Gagliardi has been fighting what he describes as a politicized justice system. Gagliardi in the 1970s rented warehouse space to Western Electric, a division of AT&T. In 1976 Gagliardi accidentally discovered Western Electric workers destroying perfectly good, unused telephone cable. He brought this practice to the attention of AT&T, which didn't seem to care. The warehouse owner finally informed the state Public Utility Commission, which launched an investigation, finding evidence that AT&T's workers routinely destroyed large quantities of new equipment. Among the destroyed property, PUC investigators learned, were 300,000 pounds of new princess phones, which workers unwrapped from their packaging and threw directly into a melting pot. Ratepayers would not only pay for this waste, Gagliardi points out, but the utility would also receive a state-approved margin of profit for each destroyed item. PUC investigators accused AT&T of fraud. For his trouble, AT&T canceled its warehouse contract with Gagliardi. Gagliardi has since been trying, without luck, to sue AT&T for breach of contract.

Gagliardi told me he believes his personal problems with the court system stem from AT&T's big-money influence on politicians. He charges that candidate Thornburgh was in AT&T's pocket, and that the global company's interests were once represented in court by current Pennsylvania governor Bob Casey.

Justice Larsen's recent charges against his fellow justice Ralph Cappy included the allegation that Cappy improperly freed former landfill operator Zdrale from prison in hopes of using Zdrale's land deal as an issue against Larsen. (Zdrale, contradicting his earlier testimony before the review board, now alleges that his attorneys and Larsen cheated him out of his thirty-five acres. He charges that Larsen promised him an additional $95,000 for the parcel. Like I said, if you think this is already too complicated, too bad.) Zdrale now alleges that attorneys Ashton and Lampl threatened him and his wife if they didn't sign over their land to the justice. He talks of a long car ride with his lawyers to the review board hearings. During the car ride, he alleges, he was subjected to threats if he told the truth. He says he had inferred an understanding that his murder case would be dropped if he protected Larsen. With a cast of characters like this, who knows? This story would keep Sidney Greenstreet and Peter Lorre guessing. Zdrale, as of May 1993, told me he's been asked to meet again with investigators.

Despite Larsen's charges, Zdrale and Gagliardi, in my presence, certainly displayed no love of justice Cappy. Gagliardi in 1987 lost a round of his AT&T contract case before Cappy, who was then serving on a lower court. While I visited Zdrale and Gagliardi, they poured over Cappy's list of political contributors, hoping to divine some clue to their legal difficulties among the hundreds of lines of contributions made to the supreme court justice. Many of the contributors to the justice's campaign naturally were lawyers and, as Gagliardi told me, "Who knows who all these lawyers are representing?"

In my mind, Gagliardi has a valid point. You shouldn't have to worry that your justice, or lack thereof, has been bought and paid for. The appointment of judges would at least remove this shade of doubt. Some say appointments will only result in more patronage and partisan decisions. At least it will get the money out of the system.

Another unhappy appellant before the state supreme court is former president judge of Cambria County Joseph O'Kicki, who in December 1989 was convicted on minor, almost humorous corruption charges. (I wrote about O'Kicki's case at some length in my book *Maybe Four Steps*.) O'Kicki, while he was still president county judge, spoke openly to reporters and writers about the purchasability of Pennsylvania's justice system. The sitting judge spoke of once carrying $10,000 in bribe money to a state attorney general, of carting political slush funds for the Cambria County Republican committee, as well as vote buying and case fixing. Even so, the attorney general's office never offered the judge a plea bargain in exchange for his testimony. (No wonder, since O'Kicki would testify about events in the state attorney general's office and the county Republican committee.) Nor was the sitting judge allowed to testify before a state or federal grand jury, an opportunity which he sought. Honest prosecutors normally jump at the chance to "roll over" a convicted judge, that is, to have him testify against others. O'Kicki was willing, but was never asked. His case, like Zdrale's, was poorly and suspiciously handled by senior deputy state attorney general Lawrence Claus.

Cambria County, and Johnstown are old-time coal and steel communities infamous for their eternal political putridity. The state attorney general's office seems to have an interest in looking the other way and actively ignoring complaints. Local reporters complain that one sitting county judge, for example, is widely known to have long-standing ties to an amusement company now under investigation for alleged illegal activities. One of the gaming company owners until recently worked at the courthouse. Johnstown bar owners say state police for years attempted to arrest perpetrators of illegal gambling. The game operators were always tipped off by a phone call from the county courthouse before the police could arrive. When the amusement company finally was raided by police, evidence is said to have been found which allegedly links a community father or two to the gaming operation. Still, one reporter told me, the state attorney general's office narrowed the time frame and focus of the investigation to exclude the prominent.

When asked about the suffocating corruption in Cambria county, attorney general Ernie Preate told a local reporter he had cracked down on all known evil-doers by going after O'Kicki. Why then had he never sought O'Kicki's testimony about alleged misdeeds? the attorney general was asked. Preate bristled that the judge was a "flake" and ended the discussion. Most prosecutors don't hesitate to use court testimony from the likes of gangsters, drug dealers and killers; AG Preate refused to hear evidence from a duly elected sitting judge. What must Preate fear will reach the delicate ears of the public?

Unevenhanded justice like this leads people like O'Kicki to believe they are politically singled out for selective prosecution. The state supreme court denied O'Kicki's request for appeal. Prosecutor Claus unwisely planned to imprison the former judge in the same prison where O'Kicki had remanded many violent criminals. O'Kicki fled the county. At this writing he is living in self-described exile in Slovenia, part of former Yugoslavia. His claim of political prosecution can, according to Slovenian law, prevent his extradition. Things are so bad in Pennsylvania that O'Kicki has become our first political refugee.

This development seemed to greatly anger and embarrass AG Preate. When asked by a Johnstown reporter whether he would at last cut a deal with O'Kicki in return for the former judge's testimony, Preate again refused, now saying he wouldn't take testimony from anyone who'd fled the country. Preate didn't explain why he hadn't sought O'Kicki's testimony *before* the convicted judge lost his appeal and fled. Preate acts with iniquity and leaves the impression he's not up to his job. No wonder many have lately expressed concern about him.

I began an ongoing fax, telephone and mail communication with O'Kicki in March 1993, the day after he became a fugitive. The former judge requested from Slovenia that I help him attain an appeal before the state supreme court. I said I would try to help, but explained I feared prospects were slim, as the court was hamstrung with problems of its own.

O'Kicki suffers from congestive heart failure and colon cancer. One of Pennsylvania's judges now faces a fugitive's death on foreign soil. O'Kicki ironically has one thing going for him. Unlike us, Slovenians enjoy a very good health care system, uncorrupted by big-money interests, politicians, lobbyists, lawyers and avaricious administrators. Treatment at a doctor's office or hospital in war-torn Yugoslavia costs only the equivalent of one dollar and twenty-five cents per visit.

13

Running to the Rock for Rescue

The problem with patronage, as we've seen, is that it's not the best way to conduct government. It's inefficient, and it's unfair. We should at least get a fair shake from government, without favoritism. This is particularly true of our court system. There can be no inside track to justice, and no perception of an inside track. One-sided justice is no justice at all.

I kept thinking about justice Rolf Larsen's accusations. He alleged that his colleague, justice Stephen Zappala, "fixed" and "steered" cases to the benefit of Zappala's bond underwriter brother Charles. I kept thinking about the language Larsen used in his accusations.

Larsen charged that Zappala at various times had met ex parte with representatives of various government bodies, and advised them the "'route' and procedures to use in prosecuting" their cases in "this court." When these suits were filed "in the manner in which justice Zappala had counseled and directed, justice Zappala then took charge and 'guided' (these suits) through the Pennsylvania Supreme Court in a 'special' manner." These various cases, Larsen wrote, resolved in favor of the governmental bodies, and against the plaintive, "with the result that (the governmental bodies') financial strength was maintained and thus the bonds that had been handled through justice Zappala's brother... were rescued from risk and maintained their strength."

I became interested and concerned about the case in which observers said justice Zappala had gone to bat for the turnpike. He'd issued an unusual "quick" court order and accelerated a hearing through the high court.

I asked one observer about the case. We hadn't spoken for several months. In the intervening months Larsen had popped his accusations and a grand jury sat listening to his complaints. The observer expressed the opinion that Larsen's charges "rang true." Justice Zappala, as far as this person was concerned, had been improperly involved in a turnpike case. What was the name of the case that troubles you? I asked.

"I'll tell you only this: the case involved the turnpike's Mid-County Interchange project." I thought I heard tremors of grand juries and investigations shaking the voice. After some prodding, I learned a little more. The case involved a contractor. Turnpike commissioner James Dodaro, I was told, communicated privately with Zappala about this case. Dodaro was justice Zappala's former law partner, and he'd pushed the justice's brother to underwrite turnpike bonds. Dodaro instructed the turnpike's legal department to appeal the case directly to justice Zappala, I was told. Those close to the case were told that the justice would be expecting the call.

The turnpike's $85,600,000 Mid-County Expressway Connection project, in suburban Philadelphia, was financed by "Series A" bonds floated by Russell, Rea & Zappala in 1986. The project began in early 1990 and was scheduled for completion in late November or December 1992, the turnpike's 1992 bond prospectus promises. The project in fact was nearly one year behind schedule. The turnpike and its underwriters in April 1989 had promised investors the interchange would open on January 1, 1992. A delay caused by several lawsuits, and the delay's sudden resolution in court, is at the heart of the story.

"This project provides a direct connection between the Mid-County Expressway (Interstate Route 476) and the Pennsylvania turnpike system," reads the '92 prospectus. "An interchange between these two major highways will provide the suburban Philadelphia area with additional regional roadway capacity and relieve some of the traffic growth problems in the Conshohocken-King of Prussia-Valley Forge area."

The scale and importance of the Mid-County project can be appreciated from information published in the turnpike's 1992 annual report. "In the Midst of Mid-County," reads the report, "turnpike engineers face many challenges." I'd learn that the turnpike's legal department also faced challenges with the project's timely completion.

"Groundbreaking ceremonies for the new Mid-County Interchange in Plymouth Township, Montgomery County, took place in late 1989," the '92 annual report explains. "Since then, construction on the estimated $70 million project has proceeded on schedule." Nothing here is mentioned about the lengthy legal delays *before* groundbreaking.

"Mid-County Interchange is situated close to the existing Norristown Interchange (#25) in suburban Philadelphia," the report continues. "The new interchange will be part of a 21.5-mile stretch of Interstate 476 linking the Blue Route with the Pennsylvania turnpike's mainline and Northeast Extension. The project extends eight-tenths of a mile or 4,500 feet on the turnpike's mainline and four-tenths of a mile on the Northeast Extension.

"The project includes the largest single contract awarded by the Pennsylvania Turnpike Commission to date. The Mid-County Interchange will be the largest interchange on the entire turnpike system. Scheduled for completion in late 1992, turnpike engineers project the average daily traffic volume during the opening year at 20,000 to 22,000 vehicles daily.

"A $55 million general construction contract for the new Mid-County Interchange was awarded to Hull Corporation of Syracuse, New York in late 1989. It includes: construction of the toll plaza, utility building, roadway, structures, signing and lighting.

"Mid-County is the first additional interchange on the turnpike's mainline to be constructed since completion of the Scranton Interchange on the Northeast Extension in 1957. The interchange will have the largest toll plaza on the turnpike with a total of 17 lanes for entering and exiting traffic and eight access ramps comprising 4.4 miles." The annual report makes no mention of an interesting fact: the contractor, originally, was not the Hull Corporation. The process leading to the contract award to Hull illuminates problems at the turnpike, and in our state courts.

Funding for this project, incidentally, included the "acquisition and construction of a new eastern regional office," which would be purchased for $2 million plus change through associate executive director S. Michael Palermo's former real estate colleague.

In January 1989, the turnpike advertised for bids to construct highway structures for its "single largest contract" on what it called its Blue Ridge project, part of the Mid-County Interchange. The job was a link in a bustling corridor of interconnected turnpike work funded by the massive $807 million RR&Z bond issue of 1986. It was an especially vital link since it promised to bring in more tolls by connecting to busy I-476. Work was scheduled to begin in the fall of '89. Six contractors submitted sealed bids on April 12, 1989. The same day the commission announced the low bidder: G.A. & F.C. Wagman, Inc., with a bid of $57,944,787. The second lowest bid, from the partnership of Dick Enterprises and Tony DePaul & Son, came in $561,254 higher.

Wagman, of York, in south central Pennsylvania, is a family-owned contracting business. It was founded in 1908 by George Aloysius Wagman, who started out as a sole laborer, hauling stone by hand, building several small bridges over creeks and canals. The next year he took in his brother. George was joined in 1935 by his son, Francis C. "Bud" Wagman. The firm worked on the turnpike back in the late 1930s. It recently built such projects as the sprawling I-95/I-395 bridge over the Patapsco River, near Baltimore's Inner Harbor, and the new Columbia-Wrightsville Bridge over the Susquehanna at Route 30. Landing the big Mid-County turnpike job was a coup, but before the contract could be awarded several complications arose. At the time they seemed like minor complications.

The company's bid had to comply with a new women and minority sub-contractor law, called MBE/WBE, for Minority Business Enterprise and Women Business Enterprise. The statute was designed to facilitate the hiring of disadvantaged firms. The newness of the law made it somewhat subject to interpretation. Before Wagman could be awarded its contract the state human relations commission paid a visit to the company to review its hiring procedures. The Office of Minority Business and Women Business Enterprise finally ruled that Wagman was in compliance with the new law. Then another obstacle presented itself. The new interchange would destroy wetlands. The turnpike found itself forced to build replacement wetlands, threatening further delay. Planners from Wagman, eager to win the job and get on with the project, met with turnpike officials to suggest ways to proceed while wetland concerns were addressed.

Despite these delays, it seemed to Wagman that it was working with the turnpike to smooth out the wrinkles. One participant remembers the perception that Wagman "was on the same team as the turnpike." The firm assumed it would win the job.

The contract was scheduled to be awarded by a vote of the commissioners in a public meeting on June 9, 1989. The day before the scheduled vote, on June 8, the second-lowest bidder, the joint venture of Dick/DePaul, along with one its minority subcontractors, filed suit in commonwealth court seeking an injunction to stop the award. The competitors claimed that Wagman was in violation of the women and minority hiring law, an issue which Wagman officials thought had been resolved.

The turnpike unsuccessfully tried to have the case dismissed. It argued that Dick/DePaul was a disappointed bidder, and so legally had no standing to sue. On June 21, 1989, the turnpike filed a pre-hearing brief in opposition to Dick/DePaul in which the commission maintained Wagman's bid was proper and that the public interest favored awarding the contract to Wagman. "Greater injury will result to the public if the (Dick/DePaul) injunction is issued," the turnpike argued, "since it will act to delay the construction of the Blue Ridge Project, a project intended to alleviate traffic congestion around Philadelphia."

The judge disagreed with the turnpike. The next day, June 22, after hearing testimony, the presiding judge, Paul Lehman, of Lewistown, granted Dick/DePaul its temporary injunction.

Observers close to Wagman remember this court hearing as almost tragic-comedy. Judge Lehman was born in 1904, retired from the bench in 1972, and served by special appointment of the court. One afternoon at about 3 p.m. Lehman announced that he could only hear arguments for another half an hour or so, as he had to catch a bus home "to Mifflintown, or someplace," as one observer remembers. A delay of weeks, even months, could be expected. Judge Lehman asked the turnpike's lawyers what the commission planned to do. Turnpike solicitors, fearing endless delay, responded that the commission planned to award the job to Wagman. Oh no you're not, Lehman told them. The judge said he wanted to hear the whole case, no matter the delay, and with his injunction enjoined the turnpike from awarding the job to Wagman. More testimony could be heard almost three weeks later, on July 13, Lehman ruled.

Turnpike planners now feared that thrashing out the disputed minority hiring law in court might delay the important Mid-County project indefinitely. The turnpike after all was pressed to complete the vast interconnected expansion projects — of which the Mid-County interchange was a crucial link — as promised to all those buyers of its bonds. Turnpike executive director Louis Martin took what he thought was the simple way out. On July 27 he altogether rejected the first round of bids, arguing that the turnpike was free to pursue its own best interest, which was to get the job moving. In early July the commission called for the project to be rebid. New bids, the turnpike notified potential bidders, would be accepted on September 12, 1989. The project was already set back five months.

For Wagman this was turning into the state contract bid from hell. Observers close to the contractor say it was badly hurt by the rejection of its bid. The year before the company committed itself to working on a $90 million bridge and road job on the nearby I-476 Blue Route. Now its resources were stretched. When it bid on the Mid-County Interchange the company was forced to pass up other jobs. Its plate was filling up, and though the troublesome bid on the Mid-County Interchange seemed increasingly shaky, the company would be legally obligated to fulfill the contract should it be awarded.

One observer close to Wagman says the company began to consider the politics of the situation. In the earlier court proceeding before judge Lehman, Wagman had been represented by an attorney with the Harrisburg firm McNees, Wallace & Nurick — considered by both the company and the turnpike as a Republican firm. The turnpike seemed to be tilted to the Democratic side. Executive director Lou Martin was a Democrat, as were Dodaro and the Zappalas. "We were aware of the connections between Dodaro and the Zappalas," one company official told me. Pennsylvanians accept as a fact of life inbred connections in government and the courts. Why not fight fire with fire? Perhaps the situation demanded a law firm with Democratic "connections," Wagman was advised, someone who "knew their way around." The company was referred to the Philadelphia attorney

David Fineman, of Fineman & Bach, because, as someone explained it to me, "there had been a prominent Democrat on the legislature named (Herb) Fineman a few years back. Maybe there wasn't even any connection there." It turns out, I'm told by a member of the firm, there is no relation between Herb and Dave Fineman. There seems to be a slight comedy of errors here.

The new attorney counseled Wagman to wait until the job was rebid and then, if necessary, take the turnpike to court. Company officials all the while feared Wagman had diminished chances for winning the rebid. In a situation where a job is rebid, the competition knows the previous low bid, which now becomes the benchmark for the new bidding. The chances of twice grabbing the golden ring are diminished.

Making matters worse, specifications for the second bid were not identical. The turnpike had rewritten the women and minority hiring requirements to make the language more clear and, hopefully, to avoid the snafu experienced the first time around. Also differing from the first bid, the contractor must now construct a noise wall. Most importantly, a $4 million bridge was taken out of the project. The delay in the start of the interconnection was becoming crucial, observers remember. More than six months had elapsed since the start of the first round of bids. The completion date for the project — if everything went right — now was delayed an entire year. The turnpike, already hurt by delays and pressed to complete the complicated, interconnected roadway as promised to investors, took a bridge out of the bid. The commission negotiated with a Pennsylvania Department of Transportation contractor to build the bridge.

"PennDot was working on the adjoining I-476 part of the project," one participant remembers. "The turnpike's contractor was supposed to do the fill work for the bridges. The lawsuits tied all that up. So the bridge had to be turned over to PennDot."

The turnpike's official explanation for granting PennDot responsibility for building this bridge was that the rebidding and subsequent rescheduling problems created harmful delays for PennDot. Interestingly, nowhere in court records does the turnpike indicate how badly the commission and its investors may have been hurt by delay. Or, for that matter, how badly turnpike investors might be hurt by continued delay.

Wagman officials and their attorney attended a gut-wrenching pre-bid hearing at turnpike headquarters on August 22, 1989. Sensing the difficulties of winning the second round of bids, the company decided to immediately take the turnpike to court.

On August 30, 1989, Wagman asked commonwealth court for an injunction to stop the rebidding and prevent the accepting or opening of the second round of bids. The court was also asked to review the legality of the turnpike's having tossed out the first round of sealed bids. Wagman would be irreparably harmed if the injunction wasn't granted, its attorneys petitioned. Commonwealth court judge Doris Smith set a hearing date in September at the Robert N.C. Nix, Sr., Federal Building in Philadelphia.

The turnpike on September 8 argued that Wagman had no standing to sue since the contractor was not holding enough bonds and so was merely a disappointed bidder. The commission attorneys cited a 1985 statute which claimed that the turnpike couldn't be sued unless the litigant held at least ten percent of outstanding turnpike bonds.

"It was ridiculous," one participant remembers. "They were saying you had to be holding $50 million in bonds out of a total of $500 million in turnpike bonds before you could take them to court!" (Others say the turnpike was misreading this statute, that it was meant to apply only in the event the turnpike went into default.) Even so, before it showed up in court, Wagman bought some turnpike bonds. "No where near $50 million worth," I was told.

This cited requirement (Turnpike Commission Organization, Extension and Toll Road Conversion Act, 36 P.S. §14[b]) states that a potential litigant in "the event of default" hold "not less than ten per-centum (10%) in principal amount of the bonds then outstanding" before the turnpike can be taken to court. This requirement becomes particularly interesting when one remembers that the principal bond dealer is Russell, Rea & Zappala. Today there's more than a billion dollars in outstanding bonds. One tenth of that is at least $100 million in bonds. If one assumes that underwriters receive a lowball commission of 1.3 percent in fees for bonds underwritten, the investment companies conceivably stand to earn $1.3 million should one desire enough bonds to take the turnpike to court. This situation is made all the more untenable when one remembers that the Zappalas' childhood friend, James Dodaro, is a turnpike commissioner. It is made completely ludicrous when one considers that the chief bond underwriter's brother and the commissioner's former law partner is a state supreme court justice, where a lawsuit potentially could be decided. And that's precisely where this suit ended up — in the lap of justice Stephen Zappala. But I'm getting ahead of the story.

One observer made the case to me that RR&Z would not make money whenever a potential litigant is forced to buy bonds. As chief underwriter, RR&Z made its profit selling turnpike bonds to other brokers when the deal was first cut, and would not profit from subsequent public sale of the bonds, I was told. I pointed out that RR&Z also handled the remarketing of bond issues. If potential contractors (or litigants) thought they must purchase $50 million or more in bonds to protect their standing in the event of court action, the supply of remarketed bonds could get tighter, increasing the value and perhaps the size of an issue, to the benefit of RR&Z.

The point is, nobody at the turnpike seemed to be considering the potential for conflict. No one seemed to consider the bounds of propriety. The great multi-billion dollar Pennsylvania turnpike was starting to resemble a back-woods family business set beside a Southern sheriff's sleepy jail: listen to this commissioner; pay his boyhood friend; if you don't like it, submit to justice from the first one's former partner, who also happens to be the second one's brother....

So Wagman bought a few thousand dollars worth of turnpike bonds to bolster its claim for standing. Events took an interesting turn in court as Wagman argued on behalf of turnpike bondholders, of which it now was one. "As a result of (the Pennsylvania Turnpike Commission's) wrongful conduct (rejecting the first round of bids)," the company's attorneys briefed the court, "(the) public, (Wagman), and other bondholders will suffer the following irreparable immediate harm: a) delay in commencement of construction; b) loss of toll revenues; c) financial loss to bondholders, (Pennsylvania Turnpike Commission), and the commonwealth."

Judge Smith on September 11 sided with Wagman. She disregarded the turnpike's assumption that Wagman lacked standing. The statute requiring 10 percent holding of outstanding bonds to bring legal action, she noted, specifically states in "the event of default."

"The core question involving standing is that a person seeking judicial resolution of a controversy be adversely affected," she'd note in a memorandum opinion. "(T)his court believes Wagman has presented evidence to show that it would be severely and adversely affected."

Smith enjoined the turnpike from opening, announcing or awarding the new bids. The turnpike was furthermore enjoined from continuing with the project until a "final disposition of proceedings filed by Wagman." The construction company was ordered to place a bond of $58,000, which it did. Here it was, almost fall, when the project was supposed to have been getting under way. Instead the interconnection was heading for another lengthy delay as commonwealth court proposed to review everything that had happened to date.

Earlier the turnpike had short-circuited a court review by simply rejecting the first round of bids. Suddenly this short-circuiting itself was up for court review. Turnpike officials decided on the ultimate short circuit.

The turnpike responded to Smith's injunction on September 13 by filing for an appeal before the state supreme court. In doing so the turnpike's attorneys claimed their appeal should operate as what's called an automatic supersedeas. State Rules of Appellate Procedure Rule 1736 provides that the "commonwealth, its officers or a political subdivision," by appealing to a higher court, automatically vacates a lower court's unfavorable ruling, as the appeal "shall operate as a supersedeas in favor of such party." In other words, simply by appealing to the supreme court, the turnpike claimed the right to disregard Smith's order and so award the contract. The turnpike notified seven bidders that on Monday, September 18 it would open and announce the bids. "Wagman was notified by the (turnpike) that its appeal to the supreme court constituted an automatic supersedeas and that the rebids would be opened as planned by the commission irrespective of this court's order," Smith later wrote.

A telephone hearing was held between judge Smith and the two parties on Friday, September 15. Wagman filed a petition of contempt against the turnpike, seeking to eliminate what it called the "alleged" automatic supersedeas. Wagman argued, and Smith would agree, that the turnpike had no right of automatic supersedeas. By statute (42 Pa. C.S. §102), and precedent, judge Smith found, the turnpike "is defined as an 'independent agency' as contrasted to the commonwealth or one of its political subdivisions." The turnpike was not the governor or a state agency, Smith ruled. It could not invoke the supersedeas. The practical reasoning for the finding was obvious: Wagman had demonstrated it would be hurt if the job was rebid, and any hearings would be made moot if the turnpike went ahead and awarded the job.

On Monday, September 18, the day the turnpike planned to open the bids for the late job, Smith filed an order eliminating the turnpike's claim of automatic supersedeas and reaffirming her September 11 injunction.

So the awarding of the contract, and therefore the project, came to a grinding halt. For most other parties this court obstacle might have proven insurmountable and costly. The turnpike simply played its trump card.

Three days before Smith's order, the day of the phone hearing, Friday, September 15, executive director Louis Martin began conferring with the turnpike commissioners, including Dodaro. In the event Smith ruled against them the following Monday, turnpike officials wanted to be prepared to immediately have her overruled so the bids for the jinxed Mid-County job could be opened.

Observers say that Dodaro and Martin agreed, should Smith make it necessary, to have the turnpike appeal the elimination of the automatic supersedeas directly to supreme court justice Zappala. They would out-gun judge Smith. This would cut costly delay. Those familiar with this case say it is their understanding that Zappala received a private communication about the situation by way of commissioner Dodaro over the weekend of September 15 to 17, 1989. An *ex parte*, or one-sided, communication is the very offense for which Zappala had voted to reprimand his colleague justice Larsen.

The next Monday Smith issued her opinion reaffirming her injunction and eliminating the turnpike's automatic supersedeas. "It is ordered that the appeal filed by the (turnpike)...shall not operate as an automatic supersedeas." Smith intended to stop the turnpike cold.

In case of this eventuality, higher-ups had already instructed the turnpike attorney handling the case to telephone justice Zappala's office and ask that judge Smith be overruled. It was the understanding of a key participant in the case that Martin had received these instructions from Dodaro. The turnpike legal staff was informed that justice Zappala would be expecting their call, a participant told me.

Justice Zappala's clerk took the call from the turnpike's legal department. Zappala's clerk requested "a piece of paper, a motion to work with," which was quickly delivered. Stephen Zappala, as planned and promised, put the case on a fast track. On September 18, the same day as Smith's order eliminating the supersedeas, while confused contractors waited at turnpike headquarters to present their bids, Zappala conducted an expedited hearing over the phone. Lawyers for the turnpike and Wagman offered oral arguments during the conference call. (The entire turnpike legal staff, I'm told, overheard this phone hearing.) That same day the justice issued an order reinstating the turnpike's automatic supersedeas, revoked by Smith. Before the order could be issued Zappala's office demanded a brief from the turnpike, which created a slight problem. The brief and its amendments by this time had grown to about an inch thick and the turnpike staff faced a logistical problem getting it to Pittsburgh. Before the end of the day the brief was delivered, and so was Zappala's order. The turnpike now was allowed to accept, open and announce the second round of bids. "Zappala wasn't stupid," one party remembers. "He allowed the turnpike to open the new bids but ruled it couldn't award the job until the full court heard the case."

"There was a big ruckus back and forth between judges Smith and Zappala," another participant remembers. "It was the most unusual bid day I'd ever seen. Bidders for the contract were told to bring their bids to the turnpike offices, where they sat in a lobby from 10 a.m. to 3 p.m., while Zappala held his phone hearing."

The obstacle of judge Smith's stay of the automatic supersedeas removed, the new bids received and opened, the turnpike's lawyers on October 18 filed for an expedited appeal before the full court. The expedited hearing was granted, and heard on October 23. (The turnpike's attorneys had not earlier asked Zappala for a full, expedited hearing because, for all they knew, Wagman might again turn out to be the low bidder, thus eliminating the need for further litigation.)

Everyone seems to agree that justice Zappala helped move things along. By the time the full court would rule on the case the turnpike would have a low-bidder in hand, prickly matters such as the contractor's MBE/WBE qualifications would have been investigated, and the commission would be ready to make the award. In contrast, when judge Lehman, independent of the turnpike, had to catch his bus to Mifflintown, the turnpike had to fear endless delay — as do most litigants before the courts these days.

It had been very quick justice. "By the time the case was heard before the full supreme court it was so messed up no one could understand it," one participant recalls. "Chief justice Nix couldn't understand why Wagman was there. He said, 'You are low bidder.'" Nevertheless, the full court decided in favor of the turnpike on October 31. The state's highest court, without issuing an opinion, vacated all of Smith's earlier orders on the unexplained grounds that Wagman had no standing to file suit. How unfair is all this? The turnpike originally fought Dick/DePaul's court intervention on the grounds it had no standing to sue, a contention that judge Lehman (and later Smith) disregarded. If Wagman and the turnpike had fought Dick/DePaul before Zappala, presumably the court would have ruled Dick/DePaul had no standing, and Wagman would have won the contract.

But that's not how it happened. The contract was awarded, as the turnpike's 1992 annual report notes, to the Hull Corporation of Syracuse, New York. It was not the smooth award the annual report would have us believe. The story of the one-year delay is mostly the story of a big snarl the turnpike suffered at the hands of the state court system, and a smoothing over the turnpike enjoyed when justice Zappala intervened.

Judge Smith, for her part, on October 25, 1989, filed a six-page memorandum opinion explaining the reasoning, and citing precedent, behind her actions. In defending her judgments she casts suspicion on the way the state supreme court, and so Zappala, handled the appeal. In her memorandum Smith reiterates her opinion that the turnpike is not a governmental body subject to automatic supersedeas. She brushed aside the assumption that one must buy bonds before suing the turnpike. "Substantial legal questions have been raised in this proceeding primarily relative to the (turnpike's) right to reject the first bid," she summed up. "...The legal questions thus raised by the evidence presented at hearing satisfy the criteria for issuance of a preliminary injunction." Unfortunately for Wagman, the turnpike had luckily found a higher judge who disagreed with Smith.

The project, the schedule, all those bonds, were back on track. Several people told me they were troubled by the expedited nature of the turnpike's successful appeal. One described the speed of Zappala's intervention as very unusual. "Sure," this observer said facetiously, "this sort of quick order happens all the time." Most troubling was the understanding of those involved that justice Zappala had received an *ex parte* communication about the case, and the equally troubling assertion that turnpike attorneys had been told that Zappala would be expecting their call. This case has the potential to lend credence to Larsen's charge that Zappala "steered" cases in a special manner to help his bond underwriter brother's clients — in this case Charles Zappala's biggest client, the Pennsylvania turnpike.

In the Wagman case, turnpike officials (including Dodaro) figured out a way to get past judge Smith, and Dodaro's patron and former law partner, justice Zappala, willingly enacted the plan. Judge Smith, in her memorandum opinion, shot back at the high court, writing that someone's rights had been trampled.

Why, I wondered, had the turnpike found it necessary to bring justice Zappala into the case? Could this have benefited the justice's brother Charles, who sold the bonds for the stalled project? At various times through the years the turnpike's legal staff have called state supreme court justices for emergency rulings, such as the call to chief justice Nix to keep embattled Peter Camiel on the commission. The supreme court is supposed to be open at all hours for emergency appeals. Why was justice Zappala selected to rule in this Wagman case? Why hadn't Dodaro and Zappala recused themselves? Perhaps as important, why wasn't the turnpike sensitive to the appearance of conflict this might present?

One turnpike official with an interest in the proceedings attempted to defend and play down justice Zappala's involvement. Charles Zappala's firm, the bond underwriter, wasn't threatened monetarily by the snafu with Wagman, this party argued. The Mid-County Interchange project, underwritten for $85,600,000, was only a small piece of the huge, nearly one billion dollar 1986 bond float, I was told. The difference in bids between the two contractors, furthermore, in the event of a court opinion unfavorable to the turnpike, might have been no more than $5 million — again, in the scheme of things, small change, I was told.

What about the element of time? I asked. Supposing, instead of the month or so it had taken justice Zappala and the full court to dispose of Wagman, the case had stretched out for years, as usually happens in courts these days? Might the project have been delayed indefinitely? In April 1989, the turnpike's revenue forecasters promised investors that the interchange would be "opened January 1, 1992." The 1992 prospectus for bonds sold by Charles Zappala's firm had to promise that the Mid-County Interchange would be "operational by the end of 1992." Might a fouled-up interconnection have driven away potential buyers of bonds, and so commissions to Russell, Rea & Zappala?

One turnpike official tried to assure me that investors would have understood a drawn-out delay. The women and minority hiring regulations at the heart of the dispute were newly written and so the court delays would probably have been understandable to investors. This person tried to play down justice Zappala's involvement in the case. Closeness to a particular justice merely means access, I was told. You simply know where to reach a particular justice. Say, over the weekend.

An observer close to Wagman questions this explanation. "We had to wonder why all these lawyers were trooping to Pittsburgh to see

Zappala when there were other justices."

A turnpike official offered a cryptic explanation. This person pointed out that lawyers often view the process of court appeals in a strategic sense. "If opposing lawyers are more experienced you might have to do more things." A less-experienced opponent makes the game easier. This person at first said it was proper for commissioner Dodaro to have involved himself with consultations to bring in justice Zappala. When pressed, this person seemed unusually sensitive and not forthcoming about the roles played by the two long-time friends.

Another turnpike observer provided an insight into this "strategic explanation" of turnpike behavior in the Wagman case. (Judge) "Doris Smith gave us a bum deal," in the Wagman case, this person explained. "It appeared Smith was wired the other way," I was told, meaning that judge Smith seemed to unfairly favor Wagman over the turnpike. Here's where partisanship begins to show itself at the turnpike, and in our justice system. I was told that turnpike officials initially viewed Wagman as a Republican firm, as the contractor in some matters was represented by the Harrisburg firm McNees, Wallace & Nurick. The partisan view of the case was further reinforced when Wagman hired Fineman, believed to be a Democratic firm. Again, perhaps a comedy of errors. A few of the Democrats at the turnpike, those close to Dodaro and the Zappalas, viewed Smith's unfavorable rulings in the light of party politics.

Judge Smith displayed apparent favoritism in several ways, I was told. For example, Smith received a post-hearing suggestion, meaning a communication after the hearing, from Wagman's attorney. One participant described the communication as an *ex parte* letter written by Wagman's attorney to judge Smith. This shouldn't, and usually doesn't, happen. Then there was the matter of her staying the automatic supersedeas, which further maddened the turnpike's legal staff. In the early 1980s, in connection with efforts to keep Peter Camiel on the commission, the turnpike had successfully invoked the supersedeas.

All this angered turnpike executive director Martin, I was told. "Lou Martin sometimes has a big ego," one observer explained. "He had ordered the rebidding of the project and he was mad that

Wagman had defied him and had gone to court, and he was upset with the way judge Smith had treated the turnpike."

This view seemed to set the stage for party one-upmanship. As an observer explained, "It's common knowledge that Dodaro is close to justice Zappala." If the Republicans (or was it the Democrats?) could "wire" judge Smith, the turnpike could just as easily "wire" the state supreme court. "Didn't they know we had a wire on the supreme court?" a participant put it. "Didn't they know who we were, what our power was?" By using Dodaro to call in justice Zappala, this person explained, turnpike officials were hauling out their big stick, playing a trump card, sending a message to others, including judge Smith, not to play procedural games with the turnpike in the future. Another message was sent to Wagman, which was viewed as trying to play partisan politics in the court system. "Don't use politics against us," was the message to Wagman and others. "Because we can use politics too, and we can beat you at that game."

Judge Smith apparently got the message, this person told me, as she ruled favorably on the next turnpike case before her. "I don't know whether someone spoke to her," I was told, "or if she simply got the message by seeing how the Wagman case was handled."

All this is bad enough, but should we let the turnpike, Dodaro and the Zappalas off the hook so easily? A deeper explanation of the turnpike's behavior might well lie in the question of whether the Mid-County Interchange would have been delayed by endless court litigation. Plain and simple, might a court delay have cost Charles Zappala money?

What about the money nobody wants to talk about, anyway? Let's say it's true that the difference in contractors was small potatoes, "only" $5 million. What was the potential loss of toll revenues? Upwards of $1.1 million for every year the interchange remained unproductive, according to turnpike projections. Other costs are less clear. What about the cost of borrowing all that money while the whole shebang is held up in court? What about the potential loss of investor confidence? In the real world, interminable delays in the American court system often kill projects, as we're reminded in justice Larsen's condo case (see Chapter 10). A million here, five million there — certainly, sooner or later, you have to be talking real money. In fact, the 1992 bond prospectus tells us, "Total costs for the (1986 bond float) Series A Projects are approximately $25 million above the original estimate in July 1986, due primarily to an increase in the cost estimate for the Mid-County Expressway Connection." There were problems with relocation of wetlands near the interchange, the prospectus notes. Even so, I was told, the one-year delay was mostly caused by the two lawsuits. "That's what held it up," one participant told me, referring to the court action.

One turnpike observer suggested that a prolonged court delay might well have cost the turnpike and its underwriters additional lost revenue, had not justice Zappala interceded. Federal tax law requires a governmental agency like the turnpike to spend the proceeds of a bond issue within five years, or the money is subject to a tax, which would certainly cost the turnpike money. The turnpike presumably had until 1991 to spend its '86 Series A bond funds, which financed the Mid-County project. So time was of the essence. A looming court battle in late '89 could certainly have stretched out two years into '91. It happens all the time in American courts. (Justice Larsen tied up his neighborhood condo project with court action for *three full years*, from March 1984 to May 1987, until the developer went belly up.)

What if justice Zappala hadn't interceded? One observer described a cascading series of events that might well have ended with turnpike administrators and underwriters losing money, profitability, and reputations. A prolonged court delay involving its biggest interchange could lead the public to lose confidence in the turnpike. This would cause the turnpike's traditionally high bond rating to be devalued. Money would then have to be borrowed at a higher interest rate, which would cost the turnpike and its underwriters money (and profit) in future bond issues. Or, conceivably, the turnpike might have trouble peddling its bonds. Higher interest means greater risk. As we were reminded by politicians and bond courtesans in 1986, there is *risk* involved in selling turnpike bonds not backed by the state.

It is perhaps true that potential bond investors might have understood a delay of a relatively small turnpike project. This interchange was not small. It was to connect several major highways to much larger combined projects. (Including, you'll remember, the new eastern regional headquarters purchased through the associate executive director's former real estate colleague.) Any chain is only as strong as its weakest link. The uncompleted Mid-County Interchange structures could arguably have loused up the usability, read profitability, of other projects. Aunt Tilly, or a truck driver, can't drive a three-thousand mile road if a bridge is missing. Who knows the whole interconnected picture?

It became interesting to me that turnpike officials seemed to go out of their way to insist that the integrity of Russell, Rea & Zappala bonds never was threatened by court setbacks in the Wagman case (or helped by justice Zappala's intervention). Normally, when the bond-seller and the judge aren't brothers, an administrator would be quick to point out that a project's underwriters require and deserve protection from harmful delay. You're normally free to look out for your investors, free to hope aloud that they make money, free to say gobbledygook like your fiduciary responsibilities to your bondholders demand quick and timely action to complete a scheduled project. (Potentially troublesome litigation, by the way, must be disclosed by a bondseller in its prospectuses.) Even Wagman, in its court briefing, wasn't shy in defending turnpike bondholders.

In this instance, because the underwriter's interests are so shamefully tangled with a turnpike commissioner and a state supreme court justice, everyone at the turnpike has to disingenuously pretend the underwriter's bacon is never on the line. They have to pretend none of their actions impact the underwriter — an amazing contention. Everyone involved seems uncomfortable and not eager to publicize that money's on the line. (Writer Steven Dickson, of the industry paper The Bond Buyer, complained to me that Russell, Rea & Zappala's representative threatened to sue the publication while Dickson was preparing his article on the problems of the justice and the investment house. RR&Z has threatened to sue at least one other newspaper lately, I've learned. These legal saber rattlings carry the unspoken threat that the underwriter's brother is a judge on the state's high court.)

The truth is, people close to the Mid-County Interchange project say time *was* becoming crucial to the turnpike, so much so that turnpike officials felt it necessary to call in Zappala and take a bridge out of the original bid. If there was no hurry, no problem, no *risk,* why do these things? Show me time and money, and I'll show you risk. If there was a risk, justice Zappala should have recused himself. He certainly shouldn't have taken an *ex parte* communication.

Justice Larsen alleged that RR&Z bonds were "rescued from risk" by justice Zappala. Consider this thing called risk. On the one hand, these people argue that sweetheart no-bid bond deals should be awarded because turnpike projects, not backed by the state, are fraught with risk and so are deserving of special, non-competitive treatment by trustworthy "friends" (see Chapter 8). On the other hand, when problems crop up that threaten the timely completion of the project, the same people, to protect their sweetheart bondsellers, are forced to argue that the bond holders or dealers were never placed at risk, and didn't benefit by any inside manipulation. It's risky business, or it's not. Which is it?

Time wasn't of the essence, they tell us, so it didn't matter that justice Zappala sped things along. Today's open-minded and understanding bond buyers, we're told, would have understood the delay and loss of potential revenue. Dan Cupper's 1990 history of the turnpike (the publication of which was officially sanctioned by the turnpike for its fiftieth anniversary), makes a big deal over a few months' delay of the opening of the roadway in 1940 (see Chapter 3). Politics prevented Franklin Roosevelt from officiating at a dedication, Cupper reminds us. "Bondholders began to point out to the commission that every day the superhighway remained closed was another day without revenue to retire its debt," Cupper writes. Now we're expected to believe the bondholders in 1989 have changed their stripes and don't care about delay, and suffer silence. Yet the bond dealer's brother, the state supreme court justice, bashes heads together to get the show rolling. An expedited hearing before the state supreme court implies that time is of the essence. Which is it?

It's easy enough to argue that Dodaro and justice Zappala should have recused themselves from the entire Wagman snafu. They should have. More to the point, the bonds should never have been awarded on a non-competitive basis. This would have saved everybody embarrassment.

In the case of *Wagman* v. *The Pennsylvania Turnpike Commission* we're presented with the interesting picture of a government agency run a little too much like a business, overseen with a little too much efficiency. Who knows the whole big interconnected picture? The bottom line, in my mind, is whether the billion plus dollars in bonds floated since 1986, enriching to a few, have cost ordinary citizens faith in their turnpike, their legislature and their courts. Greed ultimately destroys the greedy.

In the end, after all, the turnpike is just a road. Concrete, asphalt, rock and stone meeting earth. Not much different, essentially, from the two-lanes it replaced. What is different is the bureaucracy, the political order, behind the road. At what cost do we drive to Pittsburgh? We suffer our souls to get there in four hours.

The handling of the Wagman case appears to potentially violate the judicial code of conduct. Canon 1, dealing with the independence of a judge and appearance of same, reads:

A judge should uphold the integrity and independence of the judiciary

An independent and honorable judiciary is indispensable to justice in our society. A judge should participate in establishing, maintaining, and enforcing, and should himself observe, high standards of conduct so that the integrity and independence of the judiciary may be preserved. The provisions of this Code should be construed and applied to further that objective.

Perhaps, more to the point, since friends, associates and family of justice Zappala are concerned here, Canon 2, reads:

A judge should avoid impropriety and the appearance of impropriety in all his activities

A. A judge should respect and comply with the law and should conduct himself at all times in a manner that promotes public confidence in the integrity and impartiality of the judiciary.

B. A judge should not allow his family, social, or other relationships to influence his judicial conduct or judgment. He should not lend the prestige of his office to advance the private interests of others; nor should he convey

*or, knowingly permit others to convey the impression that they are in a
special position to influence him.*

The involvement of justice Zappala in the Wagman case certainly
gave people I spoke with the impression he could be influenced by
"family, social or other relationships," that Dodaro and the turnpike
were "in a special position to influence him."

Turnpike employees view the justice as having fixed this case.
Wagman representatives certainly are suspicious. The *Wagman*
episode convinced one observer at the turnpike that Zappala was a
high house judge, that all lawsuits against the agency must be filed in
federal, not state, court. Justice, and the perception of justice, has been
hurt.

Justice Zappala, sitting on the bench, has shown sensitivity to the
appearance of conflict where his brother's business is concerned.
Several times, when matters concerning an entity funded by his brother's bonds have come before the state supreme court, Zappala has
asked opposing counsel whether they mind if he hears the case. This
has happened "six or seven times," one attorney told me. In one recent
case involving a television reporter who was injured on the turnpike,
I'm told Zappala from the bench pointed out that his brother sold
bonds for the turnpike and asked if either party minded his involvement. Neither party at first objected. After arguments had been heard,
the TV reporter's attorney did object to Zappala's involvement. The
late objection was disregarded. "You're supposed to object at the start
of a case, *before* arguments," one attorney snickered. "Not after you
give a lousy argument."

Despite justice Zappala's apparent sensitivity, there remains the
inherent potential for the perception of conflict and unfairness whenever he hears a case involving his brother's interests. The turnpike's
lawyers aren't going to object to justice Zappala hearing a case. They
secretly feel it's to their interest that he's involved. An opposing counsel is also unlikely to raise objections. "You're not going to tell a judge
he may not be impartial," one attorney said. "If a judge is supposed to
be anything, it's impartial." By questioning a judge's impartiality
you're questioning his integrity, an action that may return to haunt

you next time you find yourself before that judge.

Zappala would be wise simply to recuse himself whenever *he* fears a perception of conflict. More to the point, the inherent conflict should have been avoided in the first place. The judge's former law partner and protégé should not have been allowed to award one of the biggest plums in state government — the marketing of billions of dollars in turnpike bonds — to the judge's brother. The unfairness and unworkability of this situation are apparent. Lax ethical standards have created a crisis of patronage.

"I guess we had a real hard time understanding what happened," one person close to Wagman told me about the loss of its bid. "We were low bidder. We felt confident we would win in the courts."

Another person close to Wagman seemed more philosophical about the outcome of the contractor's case. "You had to wonder about it," I was told. "But we also knew the whole elective court system in Pennsylvania is no good." What could Wagman do? It had lost in the state's highest court, without chance of appeal. He said the political nature of contracts awarded by Pennsylvania government, and the political nature of Pennsylvania courts, was well known, and he really wasn't surprised by the outcome. "As it was we were assaulting a mountain. We knew we'd probably lose in court."

Yes, I said, but when he went to bed at night he deserved to know he lost because of a point of law, not because the other party had an unfair advantage with the judiciary.

"Yes, that's right," he agreed, sounding surprised. Things are so bad in Pennsylvania that people often seem unprepared, even surprised, to listen to arguments for fairness and evenhandedness. "Personally," he went on, "I can't wait till we get a chance to vote on a constitutional amendment for an appointive judiciary. I'll be the first one to go down and vote for it." This person, I should point out, asked that his name not be used, since, he said, he still had business to conduct with the state. And you never know when you might have to go to court, he added.

I spoke with justice Zappala briefly as I finished this book. Our conversation came about through the help of someone acquainted with the justice and commissioner Dodaro. This intermediary was friendly toward me, and though I risk betraying his confidence, I believe the following story is pertinent.

One evening as I spoke on the phone with Zappala's friend I mentioned I was writing about the justice. This person picked up another phone and, while I listened, called Zappala. Addressing the justice as Steve, the mutual friend suggested he talk with me. I was given Zappala's office number and instructed to call in the morning. The next morning I called a clerk and asked for an interview, with no result. One evening a few weeks later, almost in passing, I mentioned cryptically to the intermediary that I feared Zappala and Dodaro might be in for some rough sledding. My friend hung up, and called back a few minutes later, saying I should try Zappala's office in the morning. I was given the name of secretary for whom I was told to ask, with instructions that I was to tell her the justice wanted to speak with me.

The next morning I followed instructions. The secretary took the message, and an hour or so later justice Zappala called back.

The justice was considerate and kind, and asked about my family. He struck me as very much the smooth politician (I don't mean that in a negative sense), in touch, his ear to the rail. I came away liking him. I, in turn, asked how he was doing. He said these were interesting times. I explained I'd been working on a book about the Pennsylvania turnpike, and the U.S. Supreme Court's *Rutan* decision. Zappala replied that was a *very* interesting subject. I did not ask about his family, but instead suggested we meet one day soon, face to face, for an interview in his office. He said he would try to find the time and would get back to me, if his busy schedule allowed. I never had the honor.

Reports, meanwhile, began to surface in the press that I was in contact with fugitive former judge Joseph O'Kicki. O'Kicki and his family, including two pre-school-aged children, were now exiled somewhere in Slovenia, and he'd asked me to help with his appeal before the state supreme court. Zappala's friend, hearing this, one day called to tell me that justice Zappala might be just the compassionate type who could help O'Kicki. When I went to visit justice Zappala I should bring up the O'Kicki case, I was told. Justice Zappala would already have been told about it, he said. I didn't have the heart to press for the meeting.

By having an elective bench we have insisted our judges become politicians. Successful politicians require certain survival skills. They must stay in touch, remain accessible, keep their ear to the rail. (Should I even mention fundraising?) These are the very traits that now are landing our judges in hot water.

The irony is that many people I spoke with regard Stephen Zappala as one of the more gifted jurists on Pennsylvania's bench. One family friend described the justice as able and always ready to help. Friends and family helped by the justice may prove to be his undoing, goes the argument. The strategy of family friends seems to be to steer attention away from the justice and place the blame for all these political machinations on the judge's bond underwriter brother Charles. Upon learning that RR&Z's PAC had donated nearly $20,000 to attorney general Ernie Preate, the family friend told me, "Charles is going to get his brother in a lot of trouble. For christsakes, Preate's *a Republican!*" He described Charles Zappala as heedless. "Charles is also in the waste management business, you know," the friend told me. He suggested I telephone RR&Z, which I did; I was connected to a concern described by the receptionist as National Waste Industries. "The mob doesn't like competition in the waste business," the friend said. "You think Charles cares? He just does what he wants. He acts like he doesn't care what anybody thinks. I wonder if he ever stops to think he might ruin his brother's career."

This explanation ignores the fact that justice Stephen Zappala obviously displayed an interest in the political deals that led to this controversy. Justice Zappala is known to have had a hand in awarding patronage to his protégé, commissioner Dodaro; and so he ultimately had a hand in extending that patronage to his bond salesman brother Charles. The whole idea behind patronage is to extend your influence and place people under your obligation. When things go well, people in your orbit benefit, and when things go bad, everyone suffers. Including the patron. That's what it's all about. This is the game that justice Zappala entered into in 1984 by pushing Dodaro for turnpike commissioner. The judge should know he cannot wed himself to Grande Dame Patronage and later espouse himself to have no interest.

Even if the justice received no direct financial benefit from the resulting no-bid bond work, his family benefited greatly. If I played a role in helping my brother get millions of dollars in business, you can bet others in my family, and so myself, would benefit. Raise the water in my family's lake, and my boat rises too. Drain that lake and my boat, too, must founder.

Younger generations have always faced a daunting task when bringing up our fathers. It often seems to the older generation that the rules have been changed in mid course. I counsel our fathers to consider, and change, the government they have built.

The careers, and the good names, they could be saving are their own.

14

A Rejuvenating Tonic

Having announced his investigation of the state supreme court, attorney general Ernie Preate in early 1993 found himself the target of a series of attack articles published by the Harrisburg Patriot-News. The Patriot, a Newhouse newspaper, is the state capital's monopoly daily. The newspaper attacked the attorney general for paying a driver more than $90,000 a year, and for demanding Tic Tac mints be kept in his car. They started calling him Ernie the Attorney. What are the motivations behind the Patriot's attacks? The Patriot is a conservative newspaper that hardly ever conducts investigations, let alone investigations of Republican state attorneys general. The talk in political circles is that the Patriot was put on its attack by Republicans who would prefer to see congressman Tom Ridge as the party's next gubernatorial nominee.

"Preate doesn't fit the mold a lot of these Republicans want to see in the governor's office," one observer told me. I asked what he meant. Many Republicans don't want to see an Italian-American governor, I finally got him to spit out. There's certainly a whiff of this in the air. Italian-Americans are now emerging as a strong force in state politics. While researching this book I ran into many who expressed Roma phobia, and I heard associated slurs, such as fear of the mob. We're expected to believe that we northern Europeans have more delicate sensibilities, more attuned to gentler pursuits, such as perfecting the blitzkrieg and soccer riots.

The Patriot next attacked Preate for taking contributions from questionable sources and assorted sleazeballs, without laboring the point that all our public servants take money from questionable sources and sleazeballs. In a similar vein, in November 1992, the

Patriot-News criticized state treasurer Catherine Baker Knoll for taking contributions from large investment houses. Every leading politician in the state is taking it from investment houses. We're going to have this problem until we publicly finance political campaigns. No one's talking about that.

Instead we get endless columns on cars and Tic Tac mints. This fallout shows how our system works: reporters are used as weapons to drop dimes on the politically out-of-favor. These reporters don't seem to be intellectually or institutionally equipped to shed light on the rotten workings of the entire system.

Being Italian, or even taking money from sleazeballs, is the least of attorney general Preate's problem. (One person I know who grew up in Scranton, Preate's hometown, sometimes visited the Preate household. Though this person never met Ernie, she fondly remembers his parents as fine, and lovely, people.) More to the point, Ernie Preate has cast himself as an old-fashioned politician with a high tolerance for old-fashioned bi-partisan backslapping corruption. Oh once in a blue moon he'll go after a fall guy. When Preate's competency and honesty is challenged, which seems to happen with increasing regularity, he'll stoop to name calling. He's fond of calling people who disagree with him "flakes" and worse. His slippery approach to politics and governing might have worked thirty years ago, but it's not working now. He seems to think Pennsylvanians are stupid, that the public doesn't know what's going on.

Preate's investigation of justice Stephen Zappala, meanwhile, seems to have missed the mark. Investigators for a while focused on the justice's various relatives who work as bond underwriters at Russell, Rea & Zappala. No evidence was found that any bond profits went to the justice, I'm told. That's really beside the point. This family has obviously stepped beyond the bounds of propriety in helping each other to public largesse. The laws on the books which allowed this to happen must be changed. Preate has not hesitated to criticize existing laws which he does not like. He's spent much time and state resources attempting to overturn reproductive health and privacy laws, for example. He presumes to tell women what to do with their bodies. Where is his moral outrage against no-bid bond patronage and legalized kickbacks, which have subjected Pennsylvania's government to paralysis, crisis and ridicule? Preate, of course, has been one of the leading beneficiaries of praetorian political contributions from sweetheart bond underwriters. He's fond of telling others how to live their lives, while his own ethical standards are low. It's the old double standard.

The problem with the Zappala case is not only one of potential lawbreaking. It's equally a problem of ethics, which no current public official, including Preate, seems clean enough to address. With the investigation of justice Zappala and his bond underwriting clan we're now revisiting the case of former turnpike controller Arthur Delinko, who legally placed public investments through his daughter. Following the Delinko affair the legislature proved unwilling and unable to address the central ethical questions. We should demand a tough law expressly preventing public officials from awarding patronage or contracts to family or business partners. We need an attorney general who'll enforce the laws already on the books, including the *Rutan* decision.

As things now stand, the perpetrators of excess are getting off the hook while the whistleblowers are threatened with punishment. Investigators appointed by AG Preate (who himself received nearly $20,000 from Russell, Rea & Zappala) soon warned justice Rolf Larsen that he would be subject to prosecution for making untrue charges in the event they can dredge up no *lawbreaking*. Too bad if it's merely an ethical sewer, with God-knows-what swimming around. Trouble is, things are so bad it's hard for an average person to judge whether something is illegal, or merely unethical. Justice Larsen had every right to ring the alarm bell. Threatening him with prosecution will prevent others from complaining in the future. Maybe that's what they want. The unfairness of this entire episode is monumental.

Even as the Harrisburg paper was merrily launching a personal attack on Preate, the Philadelphia Inquirer was riding to the attempted rescue of justice Stephen Zappala. In an amazingly one-sided series of fawning articles, the Inquirer spread it on thick by describing Zappala as a "tall, distinguished-looking man with tinges of gray at the temples." "I have never heard anybody say anything bad about him," the paper quotes a family member as gushing. The Inquirer breathlessly oozed that Zappala "wields tremendous power," that he was the de-facto chief justice who could personally swing the court. "He more or less has preempted the powers of the chief justice," one source described as a "lower court judge" told the paper. Someone else who is described as "close" to the court is quoted as saying, "Steve Zappala is running that court. Everyone in the court system knows who runs the court. Whenever we need something, we call Steve Zappala." "He is extremely intelligent," another bubbles. "He is also quite charming. His people skills are very good." Inquirer readers were told that Zappala was supported by state senator Fumo, "the powerful Philadelphia Democrat." The Inquirer loves to label its sources "powerful." The only power most of these guys have, as far as I can see, is the power to hear their voices rattle in over-blown, obscure hearing rooms. When it comes to making this state work, Pennsylvania politicians have made themselves impotent. At the same time it puffed Zappala, the Inquirer painted Larsen as nut "whose removal was likely..... They'll bounce him like a basketball." It defended Zappala by ceaselessly pointing out that many of Larsen's charges were undocumented when, in the case of courts, documentary evidence is often non-existent. A perception of injustice, words spoken outside chambers, aren't found on paper.

So we hear nothing but juvenile discussions of basketballs, cars and Tic Tac mints, charges of attempted hit-and-runs and talk of loonies.

The deeper, undiscussed problem involves the elective nature of both the courts *and* the state attorney general's office. Pennsylvania has had an elected attorney general only since 1980. The experiment has been a disaster, and the public has been wronged. The office was made elective out of fear that an appointed AG was too easily swayed by politics. This may have sometimes been true, especially in the 1970s, under governors Milton Shapp and Richard Thornburgh. There have also been many good appointments, as some have pointed out to me. Since 1980, when the office was opened to blatant elective politics and contributions, there has been one disastrous scandal after another. Pennsylvania's first elected attorney general, LeRoy Zimmerman, was accused in open court of playing a role in the same massive bribery conspiracy that caused the suicide of state treasurer R.

Budd Dwyer. Both Preate and Zimmerman refused to investigate charges that the AG's one-time chief drug investigator, Richard Guida, himself used cocaine, and accompanying allegations that Guida fixed drug cases. Guida, due to the efforts of others, finally went to jail.

One of the most outrageous breaches of public trust in the elective AG's office involved what's come to be known as the Susan Reinert murder case. Reinert was a school teacher from suburban Philadelphia. She was found murdered in the parking lot of a Harrisburg hotel in 1979. Joseph Wambaugh, a writer of police novels, early on became interested in the case, though he feared that suspects would not be arrested. Evidence turned up that Wambaugh in 1981 offered the case's main investigator, state police sgt. Joseph Van Nort, $50,000 if Van Nort would cooperate on a book, but only in the event arrests were made and the case went to court. Arrests were made, and one man ended up on death row. Joseph Wambaugh made himself rich by writing about corrupt cops. It turns out he's a corrupt writer. After sgt. Van Nort died, Wambaugh struck a deal with his replacement, state police trooper Jack Holtz. Tax evidence revealed that Wambaugh paid trooper Holtz $45,000 in 1986, the same year one of the murder suspects was convicted. Prosecutor Guida, who handled the case before his own fall on drug charges, would stay with Wambaugh in California and would see himself heroically and falsely portrayed in Wambaugh's best-selling book and a resulting TV mini-series on CBS.

It would turn out that the cops hid or outright fabricated evidence to secure the prosecution of Wambaugh's chief suspect, Jay Smith. Wambaugh seems to have decided early on that Smith should be the fall guy. Not letting the facts get in the way of a good script, Wambaugh proved to be a Hollywood boob who spreads around bribery money and manipulates the Pennsylvania attorney general's office to land a TV mini-series deal. Jay Smith ended up on death row, but was released by the state supreme court in 1992 due to "egregious" prosecutory misconduct and mishandling of evidence by the state police.

Amazing cashflow possibilities are realized when anything-goes big publishing meets venal Pennsylvania law enforcement. Wambaugh should have been investigated for bribery, but wasn't, no doubt since his prosecution would reflect so poorly on the state attorney general's office and perhaps even jeopardize lucrative sequel opportunities. Besides, who could they get to write the script? Jay Smith is now a free man who can never be retried for the murder of Susan Reinert. Was Smith an innocent man who was placed on death row, or was he a murderer set free by police misconduct? Either way it doesn't look good for Wambaugh and company. It certainly doesn't look good for Pennsylvania law enforcement.

What all this illustrates is the danger of throwing money into our justice system. It's imperfect as it is, but it's all we have. Twelve citizens on a jury who must decide. We can't let Hollywood happy endings or corporate megabucks warp what little reality we have. Damnit, it's *our* justice system, not Time-Warner's. Cash has polluted our two other branches of government, removing them from the reach of common people. We've got to try wherever possible to keep it out of the courtroom. Hollywood's meddling with reality recently topped the Reinert/Smith affair in a New York case involving Amy Fisher, an eighteen-year-old convicted of attempting to kill the wife of auto body shop owner Joseph Buttafuoco. All three TV networks quickly cranked out movies of the week, each reaching a different conclusion, depending on which of the three protagonists was paid to consult the productions.

In 1993 a Pennsylvania prosecutor decided not to charge state trooper Holtz with any crime, though Holtz had received $45,000 from Wambaugh, and though state police field regulations adopted in 1975 command that "A member shall not seek or accept any form of reward or remuneration excluding wages paid by the department as a result of his or her conduct while acting within the authority of his or her badge except as directed by the commissioner." Holtz, 45 years old, announced his retirement from the state police in May 1993, ending all possible disciplinary action against him.

Who can blame state police sgt. Holtz? What he has in common with many of the people mentioned in this book is that he seemed to regard his job and public trust as an opportunity to cash in. There are no across-the-board restrictions against selling out. Everyone seems to be grabbing a piece of the pie. We have lost our commitment to public service for its own sake. Pennsylvania has been pimped to the highest bidder.

Now we must consider whether AG Preate, himself having received almost $20,000 from the Zappalas, will obscure his own compromised position by prosecuting justice Larsen. In that event the attorney general will have proved nothing but that his office should be returned to an appointive position, free of the stain of money.

Evidence of institutional failure in Pennsylvania abounds in all corners, public and private. In the Zappala/Larsen case Pennsylvania's largest newspaper, the Inquirer, has shown itself to be more one-sided and vindictive than ever. Complaints about the Inquirer, a government-sanctioned monopoly, seem to be on everyone's lips. In the old days, decades ago, Inquirer publisher Walter Annenberg made no secret about using his paper to destroy political adversaries. Those were the days when it was said you didn't make an enemy of any man who bought ink by the barrel. Back then there was always plenty of competition to offer views opposing Annenberg's. Back then, when you'd been Annenberg'ed, you could at least cry out about the injustice.

Today the Inquirer is published by Knight-Ridder, a nationwide chain. It still displays plenty of Annenberg's vindictiveness and tendency to take sides, but now there is no competition to offer an opposing viewpoint, since the Philadelphia Bulletin folded in 1982.

The Inquirer is one of an increasing number of large, corporate newspapers given a government permit for monopoly called a Joint Operating Agreement, or JOA. Though naturally enough you seldom see objections raised in the corporate media, these agreements are raising concern around the country. The big newspaper chains lobbied for the Newspaper Preservation Act in the late 1960s, following a U.S. Supreme Court decision declaring an anti-trust violation in a Tucson case. Scared, the big chains ran for an exemption from anti-trust laws. Today there are little-publicized efforts to end JOAs, such as a 1991 bill written by congressman Carl Pursell, a Republican from Michigan. The Inquirer's recent shoddy behavior makes clear we've got to push for enforcement of anti-trust laws, which are on the books for a reason. Our newspapers won't be honest so long as they're cruising for government approval of their economic instability.

The public nationwide seems fed-up with arrogant corporate media. In the 1992 presidential election, the public's dissatisfaction with corporate media was amply and vocally demonstrated. The most heroically successful candidates, in the minds of the public, seemed to have been those who could best figure out how to elude these over-paid and out-of-touch corporate high priests of same-speak.

The public knows the game being played, and doesn't like it. A March 1993 nationwide poll of 1,703 adults published by the Los Angeles Times characterized reporters as "insensitive, elitist and out of touch with common people." Nearly 70 percent agreed with the state-ment, "The news media give more coverage to stories that support their own point of view than to those that don't."

Many respondents expressed the opinion that reporters ignore common concerns and kowtow to the powerful. Sixty-five percent said the press "looks out mainly for powerful people," while just 26 per-cent said reporters look out for ordinary people. Half said the media report things relevant to their own lives only infrequently. Sixty per-cent said those in the media have only some things or hardly anything in common with people like them.

Columnist and television commentator Hodding Carter told the Associated Press, itself increasingly without competition, that there may be some truth to the perception of elitism. "The top journalists move in packs with the affluent and powerful in Washington," Carter observed.

We have the problem in spades in Pennsylvania. Throughout Thornburgh's tenure as an overtly political U.S. attorney general, Pennsylvanians spoke of rumors that the Philadelphia Inquirer was going easy on Thornburgh because he was threatening the paper with anti-trust action.

There is a basic flaw in reasoning here. It assumes a moralistic staff of writers at the Inquirer who would do the right thing if only their poor, defenseless, megabuck, government-good-housekeeping-seal-of-approval monopoly newspaper wasn't held hostage. My passing study of the Inquirer has convinced me that the paper is quite happy with the status quo. It seems staffed with bullies who love one-sided, kick-

'em-while-they're-down fights. I would point out that people of high moral standing are not intimidated by threats from bad government. Thoreau, Gandhi, and Martin Luther King, to name a few, didn't stop writing, publishing and printing against injustice when threatened by the law. They wrote from jail.

The Inquirer's bullying has already contributed to tragedy in Pennsylvania. In 1987 state treasurer Dwyer shot himself to death at a news conference, after complaining bitterly of unfair treatment by the news media and the Thornburgh controlled justice system. Dwyer's wife, Joanne, told me that one Inquirer writer in particular "made Budd's life hell" when he was on trial. Over the years this same Inquirer reporter has earned a reputation as a print bully. One acquaintance described him as an emotional cripple who applies a standard for government officials that no human can meet. Standards for his own work, allowing himself to be used by prosecutors, and so on, aren't too high. Leaked Federal Bureau of investigation documents, published in my book *Maybe Four Steps,* suggest treasurer Dwyer was made the fall guy in a broad bribery conspiracy involving prominent members of both parties, including every state row officer, members of Thornburgh's staff, prominent legislative leaders, and two state senators who remain in office to this day. It's increasingly obvious why both parties want to forget the public suicide of Pennsylvania's state treasurer. Why has the big-money media also kept its head in the sand? The Inquirer happily printed cruel, front page photos of Dwyer blowing off his head, and called it a day.

In the Zappala/Larsen matter we see the same thing happening all over again. The Inquirer takes up the party line and casts one as a hero, one as a crazy villain, and damn the truth to be found in the objective middle ground. It's clear to most Pennsylvanians that this monopoly newspaper has become a dangerous tool for party leaders. Criminal cases are decided on a political basis, then party leaders spoon-feed the Inquirer whatever they want printed. Smaller news outlets down the line pass on and reverberate the party lies. When the drums start beating against you, you're dead. This is precisely the danger of concentrating media into a few hands. Government sanctioning of monopoly newspapers has helped to create this judge/jury/executioner climate. Newspapers should take their chances on the open market. Give them a shoe shine, welcome them to God's green earth, and let them compete like the rest of us. To survive they can cut profit margins, overhead and salaries. Maybe then reporters won't be so elitist.

The Inquirer and other big-money publications increasingly seem to be adopting the Spy Magazine brand of degrading, personality reporting. The trouble with personality reporting is that it builds up the most prominent, providing a comforting, fuzzy spotlight, while further degrading the powerless, who are made to feel insignificant and not even worthy of serious coverage. I believe the role of the writer in our society should be to aid and bring comfort to the least among us, and make uncomfortable the most secure.

The Inquirer's stock-in-trade is to label anyone who questions the party line, such as Larsen, a kook or a nut. What's wrong with that? In the late 1970s I was working with others to keep the damaged Three Mile Island reactors closed. At one community meeting a mental health professional suggested we try to have the utility executives declared mentally unfit. As promising as the idea sounded, we immediately voted it down. At the time the Soviet Union was declaring political opponents insane, and shipping them off to years of exile. Some of their best and brightest were locked up just because they didn't want to go along with the dirty mob.

When you dismiss someone offhand as a kook or a nut, as the Inquirer likes to do, you're attempting to take away their last bit of dignity. It's bad enough that average citizens today can't afford access to our legal system, or health care. Or our political system. Or that their voices are drowned in a $300,000 per minute technobabel. To dismiss someone as crazy is to attempt to deprive them of all they have left — their God-given faculties.

The offices of the Philadelphia Inquirer are barricaded in a crumbling corner of Philadelphia, with little evidence that Knight-Ridder is doing anything with its government-sanctioned profits than shipping the cash out of state.

Some of these Philadelphia Inquirer writers remind me of the kind of bullies who tormented Quasimodo in the medieval public square. They're the kind who drunkenly put down their thumbs at the Roman circus. They don't know or care about justice, or see the decay of society around them. They only want some stooge to throw down a body. A bit of merriment, a distraction from their own over-fed immorality.

It's easy enough, and popular, to place the blame for what has happened to America on our politicians, big business, and their praetorian cohort Greek chorus media. Truth be told, we the people hold the reins, and it's we who sat back and allowed this to happen to our country. It's gotten to the point where our problems sometimes seem overwhelming, almost insurmountable.

There was one more place I wanted to go. One day not too long ago I got in the car. Got a little money from the bank. I drove the Pennsylvania turnpike west, up into the Alleghenies, to the top of the mountains.

These hills that once stopped so many generations of Pennsylvanians are today only a Sunday drive for a father and a little girl. You can get out of your car and look down at the wooded valleys. It was our lack of foresight, our penny-wise-and-pound-foolishness that doomed Pennsylvania to second-rate status.

"What about Pennsylvania, anyhow?" writer Theodore Dreiser asked in 1916. "Why hasn't it produced anything in particular?" Through the centuries Pennsylvania has remained one of the most populous states in America. At the high water mark, earlier in this century, Pennsylvania's electoral college votes numbered only behind New York. As late as 1960 the census ranked Pennsylvania the third most populous state. Yet the state has produced only one president of the United States — James Buchanan — widely regarded as one of the worst. Pennsylvania's ingrained politics of patronage and unholy compromise have produced politicians that the rest of the country rightly want to avoid. We've squandered our wealth and our potential. We're fond of deluding ourselves that we're so fair and Godly. We give lip service about the common wealth. Other Americans see the government we've built for ourselves as partisan, dishonest and overbearing.

What's our problem? It's not a secret. In his 1962 book, *The Other America*, Michael Harrington wrote of an American increasingly split in two between the haves and the have-nots. Two societies, one with access to the legal system, health care, education, politics, and a decent, stable life. The other, left to rot. He argued that the cost of giving hope to people is much less than the cost of neglect. In his 1963 book, *The Fire Next Time,* James Baldwin cursed our greed and neglect and prophesized the cataclysm that today wracks our society. All that stands in the way of a just society is a vast lobby of profiteers and legally bribed office holders who are getting rich from the way things are.

We certainly have been failed by our medical, legal and insurance professionals. Everyone seems out for themselves, which is after all the example set by our leaders in government. The levers of society are increasingly moved out of reach of the average person. Not long ago the U.S. Supreme Court, in a case called *Herrera* v. *Texas,* ruled that a person on death row has no automatic right to a federal hearing or appeal, even if evidence has been found that a person is innocent. Justice Harry Blackmun dissented with the comment, "The execution of a person who can show that he is innocent comes perilously close to murder." One young law student described for me a case involving a murder conviction of a Southern black man who later learned that his court-appointed attorney was a grand wizard in the Klan. The federal courts, long the only refuge from local hatreds and peculiar ways, would send this man to death without a hearing.

Throughout the course of researching this book I heard, *ad nauseam,* people defending government patronage, cronyism and inside dealing by saying, "This is the way business does it." Well, fellas, this is not business. This is government, and it belongs to us all. We should make something special of it. We shouldn't pimp it out. I also heard continuous complaints from "public servants" who said they would do better financially in private business. Well, by all means, go into business.

At the heart of our problem are our two political parties. Noam Chomsky, the noted linguist, is fond of saying, "We have only one political party — the business party." I've tried to show in this book that the Republicans and Democrats secretly aid each other to keep the money flowing into their coffers. "They *never* do anything to stop each other's funding," one insider confessed to me. "That's the unspoken golden rule." It's really one political party, composed of a professional political class, removed from everyday realities of common people, and it's killing us. Jefferson, the revolutionary, and probably Lincoln, the preservationist, would today be debating whether the time has come to throw the Republican/Democratic party onto the scrap heap of history. We need a second party of concerned citizens who agree not to stick around forever, not to draw larger salaries than average taxpayers, and who don't view government as a professional calling to enrich themselves and their friends. And who at least want to come to work.

I expressed outrage to one old hand that library books were destroyed even as public schools were going to hell. "Library books have no political constituencies," this graybeard winked at me. "And school kids don't make political contributions." True enough. Today America practices constituency politics. We have forgotten the meaning of *Commonwealth*. We should begin again to ask ourselves how our public actions will benefit the common wealth. To do that we must eliminate the influence of big, special interest money on our government.

In the 1970s Amory Lovins spoke of a "soft path" to energy production. His point was that we waste more energy through lack of efficiency than most countries produce. It makes more sense, and is cheaper in the long run, he argued, to conserve and thoughtfully increase efficiency than to build monolithic power generation plants. The big money laughed at him then, but they're not laughing now.

We need to blaze a "soft path" in our politics. We need to get the big money out. Who can argue that we're not currently going down a dead-end street? It now costs upwards of four million dollars to run for an average U.S. senate seat (millions more in some states), and hundreds of thousands to run for congress. With no end in sight. The average elective official spends nearly every waking hour chasing political donations. Soon only Texas billionaires will be able to make themselves heard. We need to force broadcasters, who reap huge profits from *our* airwaves, to donate political time. We need public financing of elections. Some argue that it is the ultimate waste to spend public money on political campaigns. How much more public

money is wasted by awarding fat no-bid contracts to political donators?

We as individuals need to get involved. We need to come together,
and make friends. Our goals are simple and well known. It is our vital
interest to create stability at home and abroad. We need to give people
a descent shot at a home and a good life. We need to renew our social
contract between our rich and our poor, from Westinghouse to the
crack house. We need to give the average person the ability to control
his or her life with self-reliance, independence and prosperity. We
must identify society's problems and not be afraid to use government
as an instrument to cure those problems. That instrument can do no
good so long as it's so dirty.

The two hundred and fiftieth anniversary of the birth of Thomas
Jefferson was marked in 1993. Jefferson mistrusted government, but
when the time came he wasn't afraid to use it wisely. He's lately been
derided, unfairly, I think, for espousing a message that's some say is
irrelevant to us. Some see him merely as a gentrified, landed aristocrat.
I think his vision is more pertinent than ever. Jefferson called for independence and self-reliance. Today, the age of the cradle-to-grave corporation is dying. The age of the computer is already allowing many
of us to live independently of the city, free of the corporation. Still
we're hampered by antiquated zoning laws that prevent us from working and making goods at home. We should be allowed to work at
home, to conduct small-scale manufacturing at home. It's what built
Pennsylvania.

The story of the Pennsylvania turnpike, to me, is first a cautionary
tale of missed opportunity. But it's ultimately the story of opportunity
fulfilled.

Prosperity always comes at the crossroads. If you can figure out
where people are going, as did De Witt Clinton when he built the
Erie Canal, you can grab a piece of the commerce as it goes by. We
know the world is going to computerize. We in rural and green
Pennsylvania can capitalize on that, and make it easy for people to
work at home. Why, for example, can't we file state taxes by modem?
We know someday we will — why not now? Where are our public

internet networks, our data highways? We know they're coming —
why not today? These can be among the new missions for our public
libraries. Where, incidentally, are our high-speed train lines?

Our ills today certainly are great, and the praetorian defenders of
the way things are would have us believe they are incurable. T.E.
Lawrence wrote, "There could be no honor in a sure success, but
much might be wrested from a sure defeat." Often forgotten these
days is the pivotal importance of individuals. The recurring theme of
America, our great gift to the world really, are stories of individuals
who mustered courage and stood up to the black night. Our heroes
would be any other society's quixotic laughingstocks. George
Washington, the bumbling yankee doodle, hunkering down in Valley
Forge, at last taking the initiative on the icy Delaware, finding himself
as a general. Hanging in when any other man would have quit, he
freed history from monarchy. Lincoln, incapacitated by months of
deep depressions, gathering himself in Springfield. The moment he
saw beyond himself was really the moment the shackles of millions
began to break. FDR, his legs shriveled with polio, taking that first
painful step. With that step millions would walk with him to daylight.

We can once again make our country a beacon for the future. It's
not going to cost more, it's going to cost us *less*. It will enrich us. By
creating a more equitable tax system we can solve many ills and
inequities, and the spirit of trying to make things work is a rejuvenat-
ing tonic. Robert Kennedy used to say we know what we have to do,
and we know we can do it, and anything less than trying is unbecom-
ing the great people that we are.

With the 1990s Pennsylvania's state budget approaches $30 billion
a year. The national budget is over a trillion. That's real money. Do
we spend it to further enrich the few, or do we chose to spend it for
the common wealth?

What about Pennsylvania? The path of big-money politics and
insider largesse is a lonely and narrow road winding over a cliff.
William Penn's holy experiment is today barely remembered on the
lips of feuding clans, on smoky battlefields, as just another light that
failed. If it is remembered at all.

We're each of us only here for a short while. In the end, what we
stand for, who we decide to help, is how we're judged. Should we

Pennsylvanians come together with a whisper of tolerance and mutual respect, with the spirit of equality and justice on our lips, to reaffirm a calling for universal opportunity, prosperity and dignity, the world will again draw close to listen.

Our ancestors broke the fields, leveled the mountains, cleared ground for broad humanity. The inheritors of a grand past, we have an appointment to build a grander future.